# CHAMPIONING WOMANHOOD

### THROUGH A
### HIGHER CONCEPT
### OF GOD

## R. ALLAN DERMOTT

**BALBOA.**PRESS
A DIVISION OF HAY HOUSE

Balboa Press books may be ordered through booksellers or by contacting:

Balboa Press
A Division of Hay House
1663 Liberty Drive
Bloomington, IN 47403
www.balboapress.com
844-682-1282

Because of the dynamic nature of the Internet, any web addresses or links contained in this book may have changed since publication and may no longer be valid. The views expressed in this work are solely those of the author and do not necessarily reflect the views of the publisher, and the publisher hereby disclaims any responsibility for them.

The author of this book does not dispense medical advice or prescribe the use of any technique as a form of treatment for physical, emotional, or medical problems without the advice of a physician, either directly or indirectly. The intent of the author is only to offer information of a general nature to help you in your quest for emotional and spiritual well-being. In the event you use any of the information in this book for yourself, which is your constitutional right, the author and the publisher assume no responsibility for your actions.

Print information available on the last page.

Scriptures Taken from King James Version

ISBN: 978-1-9822-3408-9 (sc)
ISBN: 978-1-9822-3410-2 (hc)
ISBN: 978-1-9822-3409-6 (e)

Library of Congress Control Number: 2019912807

Balboa Press rev. date: 04/27/2023

To the women
who have inspired me over the decades
and to the men
who understand why

# CONTENTS

Acknowledgements ................................................................... ix
Introduction .......................................................................... xi

Chapter 1    Patriarchic Superstitions Versus the
              Matriarchic Goddess ............................................... 1
Chapter 2    God's Gender in the Old Testament and the
              Image and Likeness .................................................. 7
Chapter 3    Three Major Views of Women: Jesus, Plato,
              and Aristotle .......................................................... 34
Chapter 4    St. Paul's Teachings about Women .......................... 74
Chapter 5    God: Masculine or Feminine or Both? And
              What Effect This Has on Our Concept of Women .... 103

Epilogue ........................................................................... 151
Bibliography ..................................................................... 157

# ACKNOWLEDGEMENTS

To begin, I wish to thank a former colleague, Professor Diane Chin, who about fifteen years ago recommended that I read Jostein Gaarder's *Sophie's World*, a novel about the history of philosophy, a book that awakened me to the influence of Plato and Aristotle on Christian theology. In doing further research on the subject, I found women to be the greatest victim of this influence. From there my research widened, and intensified over the last ten years.

I also wish to express gratitude to my wife Lynn for being my first reader, sending me back to the keyboard to revise; my sister-in-law Diane for finding errors and offering worthy suggestions; my daughter Danica for recommendations for more research here and there and for adding a summary here and there, etc., etc., etc.; my brother Leonard for his meticulous eye for detail and proofreading quotes and for his other helpful comments; my son Drew for his contribution; and then again for Lynn's and Danica's reading the manuscript a second time after I had made all these corrections, changes, and additions. All these contributions have made this a much better book and have several, or should I say many, times saved me from possible embarrassment.

To straighten out Aristotle's research and conclusions about equality based upon the number of human and animal teeth, I wish to thank Dr. Pamela Weitzel (dentist) and Dr. Robert Furness (veterinarian) for their expertise.

For the title, much gratitude goes to two women: Jennifer Doak Carruth, Esq., for the core of the wording, and Diane Johnston for her comments in a survey which led me to modify the core a bit.

Many thanks go to Ashlyn Lembree, Esq., copyright expert, and her most capable law school student, Andrew Schmid.

# INTRODUCTION

With the harvest time of thought upon us, the various sects of the three main monotheistic, Abrahamic religions need to separate the wheat from the tares and then the wheat from the chaff—to separate the true principles that the eternal Mind of the universe has given humanity, from the contamination of ancient human hypotheses that has weaseled its way into the sacred pages and resulting cultures. There is no better place to start than with the issue concerning women.

Since humans tend to consider those ideas more aligned with their own, I too am the same way and will be focusing on the ancient syllogisms adopted into Christianity concerning women, syllogisms that have gone on to influence most of the Western world. However, I do encourage Jewish and Islamic scholars also to examine their own religions for influences of superstitions, pagan ideas (especially of Aristotle), and anti-Elohistic bias concerning women.

The purpose of this volume is to examine the most common myths about women, how they have enslaved women, and how thinkers, with God's help, can free, and are freeing, half of humanity. This ancient ignorance has expanded to include male arrogance, even to the extent that data were falsified in quasi-research "to prove" that women are inferior. But the lower-grade steel in the foundation of women's inequality has been ancient superstitions about their menstruation, conflicting ideas about the nature of God (masculine and feminine, or just all-masculine), the replacement of Christ's loving view of women with Aristotle's outrageous, diabolical views of them, and the corrupted translations of what Paul wrote about women and forgeries attributed to him. Science and critiques of faulty syllogistic thought processes in ancient documents have ripped this lower-grade steel out and left the foundation for claiming women's inequality severely unsupported. The beliefs and customs built on this foundation are the cracked walls still held up by the cement of ignorance, patriarchy, and arrogance. With the cement left in the foundation and walls exposed as nothing, the bricks that have housed feminine inequities should soon fall into the dust.

As a matter of fact, many bricks have already fallen. Patriarchic-thinking men and institutions ought to make occasional glances around and overhead. The unrighteous walls of Jericho are about to crumble again.

When the ancient Scriptures began to be translated into modern languages, particularly into English as covered here, the times were very patriarchic. Since the patriarchic thought of Elizabethan times influenced the biblical translations, which in turn have influenced many modern translations, I have chosen the King James Bible, among the first to be contaminated by patriarchy, as my main source of Scripture. This is not meant to condemn that translation, because indeed it is basically a very inspired, beautiful, even poetic, rendition. The problem is that some choice of words and some grammatical structures unnecessarily demean women. We will examine these more closely, comparing them to the original Hebrew and Greek.

Another reason why I chose the King James Bible is that James Strong's *The Exhaustive Concordance of the Bible* and his dictionaries of the Hebrew and Greek words are excellent sources for researching the influence of patriarchy on translation. Anyone who knows a Bible verse number and what word is of interest can find it and its etymology without my endnoting Strong's page numbers. The biblical references themselves are also just cited and noted in text but not endnoted.

My investigation found verifications, inconsistencies, occasional humor, and plenty of patriarchy. This adventure has been more than ten years in the planning and traveling through books and more books. The education, I believe, has made me a better man, and I have gained a better understanding of what women have had to endure for millennia. I have tried to make this experience an adventure for the reader, also. I look forward to meeting more confident women and better-balanced, understanding men.

# CHAPTER 1

## PATRIARCHIC SUPERSTITIONS VERSUS THE MATRIARCHIC GODDESS

For ancient Hebrew women, menstruation was considered just as impure and highly contagious as leprosy and unnatural discharges (Leviticus 15), discharges that seem, as described, to be from venereal diseases, especially gonorrhea.[1] So whether one had gonorrhea or menstruation, the person's clothes were contaminated, as well as any furniture used. Thus each month, in order to be declared clean again, women had to go through seven days of purification and bring either two turtledoves or young pigeons to the priests for the same sin-offerings and burnt-offerings that the venereal diseased needed to be pronounced clean. The tendency was to believe that the menstrual discharge reflected on the woman's moral purity,[2] "being a reminder that all uncleanness is hateful to God, and that He is to be glorified in our bodies as well as in our spirits."[3]

Early Hebrew culture, like all primitive societies, believed that people could be possessed of demons, or devils, or evil spirits— whatever they were called—especially if the people were in a state of uncleanness. Both the Old and New Testaments offer many examples of those possessed. But during their menstrual periods, women sometime experience varying degrees of physical discomfort or even illness and of emotional temperament. In those ages, without a scientific explanation of human menstruation, it was so easy for ignorant minds to succumb to superstitious suggestions. Women were sometimes thought more creature than human. With those women moaning in more extreme cases, or even lying in bed ill, while in their period of uncleanness, the logic of the times dictated that the monthly visitations of demons and uncleanness were a sign of these possessed, impure human creatures' inferiority.

The syllogisms of the times went something like this:

> **Major Premise**: Anyone who secretes blood is being either punished for impurity or taken over by an impure demon.
> **Minor Premise**: Women secrete blood.
> **Conclusion**: Therefore, women are impure.
> And thus:
> **Major Premise**: Anyone who is impure is also inferior.
> **Minor Premise**: Women are impure.
> **Conclusion**: Therefore, women are inferior.

For some women who were going through menopause, it was thought they were trading impurity for insanity. Ignorant, superstitious minds were dooming womanhood and the woman's human experience. Ever since science has explained woman's menstruation, civilized societies no longer believe that secreting blood is a sign of impurity or demons. Yet, the conclusions of the two syllogisms above, based on those ancient superstitions, still linger on that women are inferior.

With infidelity being higher among men than women, it is ironic that women were the ones once labeled impure. But even "the seed of copulation" was considered impure (Leviticus 15:16-18). If it got on anything during sexual intercourse, the garment or bedding had to be washed; whatever the case, the man and woman had to go into a state of purification (washing their bodies) until evening. The male's natural sexual discharge, however, was not thought to be as highly contagious as the woman's menstrual discharge. The difference that enslaved woman was that hers involved blood. James Hastings writes:

> Among all primitive races the blood, especially of human beings, has been and is regarded with superstitious, or rather, to be just, religious awe. By the Hebrews also blood was invested with peculiar sanctity as the seat of the soul (*nephesh*), that is of the principle of life (Lv 17:11 "the life [Heb. *nephesh*] of the flesh is in the blood").[4]

The idea that the blood was the seat of the soul has been with humanity for millenniums. In the Medieval Period, Christians thought that the soul loved to live in the blood, especially in the left elbow. Physicians would bleed the right arm of the sick with the hope of letting out the evil spirits but stopping the bleeding before the soul could escape. If a patient died during such bleeding—from either the sickness or the bleeding—the patient's soul had escaped.

During menstruation a woman is bleeding. Were the evil spirits draining out? Or was her soul exiting, leaving a demon behind to tempt men?

The importance of recognizing whether a woman was clean and innocent or demonic is illustrated in Samuel T. Coleridge's narrative poem *Christabel*. Though first published in 1800, it is all about medieval demonology. The daughter of Lord Roland de Vaux of Tryermaine, Geraldine (rhyming with Leoline, whose soul she was after) was a serpentine demon called a lamia but disguised as a beautiful woman. The purpose of a lamia is to avenge her wronged father by using the innocent daughter (in this case, Christabel) to capture the soul of the innocent's father (here, Sir Leoline). Sure enough, Sir Leoline was taken by Geraldine's physical beauty and at the end of the poem led forth the lady Geraldine. But in the Middle Ages, a man did not offer his right arm when leading forth a woman as a man would today. Back then he would put his left hand on his hip and extend to her his left elbow, the seat of his soul. The woman would then reach out and hold on to his soul as he led her forth. Did a man want to extend his soul to a woman who was possessed? If he ignominiously or even just ignorantly did so, he would lose it as Sir Leoline did.

Just what was exiting during a woman's menstruation—evil spirits or her soul? What was left behind to greet men?[5] For millenniums, worried men had wondered.

These superstitions about women and blood evolved with the evolution of patriarchy, which began, archaeologists inform us, about 7,000 years ago.[6] Back then, before patriarchy, a matriarchic culture ruled societies, which may have extended as far back as 25,000 B.C.E.[7] Among the idol deities, the Mother Goddess was chief. She was the source of life and gave her image, women, fertility. Some women even painted their cheeks with the red juices of fruit, symbolizing the menstrual blood of the Mother Goddess. The idea that a male god and men were the source of life was a foreign one and did not evolve until patriarchy had started replacing matriarchy over at least a thousand years. During the reign of the matriarchic Mother Goddess, women had all the rights that have been afforded men during patriarchy.[8] Women could buy and sell property (via trading) and enter into other contractual arrangements. It is amazing what decades and decades of archaeological findings have uncovered in the ground and in carved and painted ancient walls and columns. Numerous books and PBS DVDs document these findings.

This goddess took several forms. One that spread out over Old Europe and traveled to Egypt and the Middle East was the Snake Goddess. Her images saturated all of the Isle of Crete where ivory and faience statuettes show snakes intertwined around pregnant abdomens and breasts.[9] As Marija Gimbutas points out in her scholarly work, *The Goddesses and Gods of Old Europe*, "The snake was stimulator and guardian of spontaneous life energy..." and coiled about the goddess's pregnant belly, breasts, buttocks, and even knees was a sign of protection for a mother.[10]

Merlin Stone points out that the Philistine people, more cultured according to archaeology than the Bible presents them, were sea-faring and brought the Serpent Goddess from Crete, slowly introducing her to all the peoples of Canaan, including the Hebrews. This same goddess, known in Egypt as the Serpent Lady, made her way across the Sinai into Canaan, reinforcing the fertility goddess for Hebrew women.[11] She was found as far east as Babylon. As the Semite tribes transitioned from matriarchy to patriarchy, this goddess remained in Hebrew homes until the Babylonian Exile. While matriarchy was losing ground with the idea that the Great Goddess and women were the source of life, patriarchic superstitions about blood, in particular, menstrual blood, demoted women to impure, inferior, demonic helpmates across most cultures, not just the Hebrews.

As Gimbutas summarizes:

> This masculine world is that of the Indo-Europeans, which did not develop in Old Europe [where matriarchy and the Great Goddess reigned] but was super-imposed upon it. Two entirely different sets of mythical images met. Symbols of the masculine group replaced the [feminine] images of Old Europe. Some of the old elements were fused together as a subsidiary of the new symbolic imagery, thus losing

their original meaning. Some images persisted side
by side, creating chaos in the former harmony.[12]

Part of this chaos mentioned will be evidenced in our next
chapter when we cover the evolution of two Hebrew concepts of
God, one which claims both male and female as His image, and the
other, which acknowledges only men as His likeness. As we trace
the chaos caused by the Hebrews' vacillating between accepting and
rejecting the fertility goddess until idolatry was finally eliminated
and as we trace the evolution of the Supreme Being to God's most
noble presentation as both masculine and feminine by the end of
the age of the prophets about 400 B.C.E., you are cautioned to keep
the roller-coaster bar before you well in place as we roll through
the centuries.

# Endnotes
## Chapter 1

1 Frederick C. Eiselen, Edwin Lewis, and David G. Downey, *The Abingdon Bible Commentary*, New York: Abingdon Press, 1929, p. 288.

William Smith, *A Dictionary of the Bible*, Hartford: S.S. Scranton, 1868, p. 782.

Furthermore, as late as the nineteenth century, a woman referred to her menstruation in her diary as "a common disease." *History Detectives*, PBS's *World*, Boston, April 5, 2010.

2 Robert Jamieson, A.R. Fausset, and David Brown, *A Commentary, Critical and Explanatory, on the Old and New Testaments*, I, Hartford: S.S. Scranton, 1872, p. 83. (See commentary for Leviticus XV.)

3 J.R. Dummelow, *A Commentary on the Holy Bible*, New York: Macmillan, 1912, p. 94.

4 James Hastings, *Dictionary of the Bible*, New York: Charles Scribner's Sons, 1937, p. 101.

5 For example, for what Coleridge read about medical demonology and how demons could reanimate a body whose soul had exited, see John Livingston Lowes, *The Road to Xanadu: A Study in the Ways of the Imagination*, Sentry ed., Boston: Houghton Mifflin, 1964, p. 518.

6 Allan G. Johnson, *The Gender Knot: Unraveling Our Patriarchal Legacy*, rev. and updated ed., Philadelphia: Temple University Press, 2005, p. 52.

7 Merlin Stone, *When God Was a Woman*, New York: Barnes & Noble, 1993, p. xii.

8 Johnson, p. 179.

9 Marija Gimbutas, *The Goddesses and Gods of Old Europe: 6500-3500 BC*, New and updated ed., Berkeley: University of California Press, 1982, p. 146.

10 *Ibid.*, p. 95.

11 Stone, pp. 204-208.

12 Gimbutas, p. 238.

# CHAPTER 2

## GOD'S GENDER IN THE OLD TESTAMENT AND THE IMAGE AND LIKENESS

Religion has perhaps had the greatest influence in shaping the position of women in society. As matriarchy was clashing with patriarchy, the Hebrews found themselves vacillating between the two for thousands of years, between which deity was worthy of worship and among what human rights did women have. The Hebrews were also vacillating between two concepts of their chief God—Elohim and Jehovah (Yahweh)—between whether God is both masculine and feminine or strictly male, and between worshiping Asherah, the serpent goddess, or not honoring her and her promise of fertility and birthing protection. As the position on God goes, the equality of women eventually goes—even if it takes millenniums.

We will start with the Hebrews' vacillating between the deities of matriarchy and patriarchy and then move to that between Elohim and Jehovah. We shall proceed slowly through this first section, not only to show how inconsistent the Hebrews were in worshipping one God, but also, and more importantly, to prepare thought for how the worship of the goddess Asherah may have influenced the accepted nature of the One God's being feminine as well as masculine.

### Asherah

The patriarchic family in the Middle East was headed by El, the Canaanite male God, whom the Hebrews later adopted as their own, and El's wife, Asherah[1] (spelled several ways, including Ashtaroth in the Scriptures), the ancient Mother Goddess or Great Goddess, provider of fertility and childbirth for women, and symbolized by the serpent.[2] Asherah and El were said to have had a goddess daughter, Astarte, and a son, Baal.

The name Astarte is mentioned only nine times in the Bible;[3] Baal is a major player through much of the Old Testament. Asherah is referred to forty times.[4] At least two authors wrote that Astarte (a Greek goddess) is the same goddess as Asherah.[5] Astarte supposedly had a passionate relationship with her lover-brother Baal, but if Astarte is the same as their mother Asherah, then this relationship gets even more confusingly complicated. In any case, Merlin Stone writes:

> Astonishing was the archaeological evidence which proved that Her [Asherah's, or Astarte's] religion had existed and flourished in the Near and Middle East for thousands of years before the arrival of the patriarchal Abraham...[6]

Raphael Patai reports that several archaeological inscriptions paired Asherah with Yahweh (Jehovah) Himself: "These inscriptions show that in popular religion the goddess Asherah was associated with Yahweh, probably as his wife, and that 'Yahweh and his Asherah' were the most popular divine couple."[7] Thus we shall see the difference between the "popular religion" of that time and the official record of the Yahwists in the Scriptures.

As we now examine Asherah in the Scriptures, we must remember that the Yahwists naturally called her an abomination while the popular religion loved her.[8] Men tended not to oppose their wives' burning incense to this goddess for fertility and childbirth protection. As women lost their rights with the fading of matriarchy, for them fertility and childbirth became even more important. Since husbands usually died before their wives, these women had to depend upon a son to provide for them. A son was literally a mother's material salvation.

The story of the barren Shunammite woman with an old husband illustrated to women that they could rely on Elohim for fertility and childbirth. Furthermore, when her son was grown but died because of some problem with his head, Elisha restored her son and thus her material salvation. The story counters the idea that women could not rely on God for fertility and childbirth but must burn incense to a goddess, an idol. (See II Kings 4:8-37.)

Nine hundred years later, Jesus copied Elisha's restoration. As he and his followers approached the city Nain, "there was a dead man carried out, the only son of his mother, and she was a widow." She was grieving not only for the loss of her son, but also for the loss of her financial future. Jesus had compassion on her and first went to her to comfort her. Then after raising the man from the dead, Jesus "delivered him to his mother." The Hebrews had not worshiped the fertility goddess for over five hundred years, but this story illustrates again that God provides for the widow. (See Luke 7:11-16.)

## Vacillating Between Asherah and Yahweh in Hebrew History

Now let us trace Asherah through Hebrew history. When Moses' right-hand man Joshua went the way of Moses to the afterlife about 1425 B.C.E., the children of Israel rebelled (Judges 2):

> 12 And they forsook the Lord God of their fathers, which brought them out of the land of Egypt, and followed other gods, of the gods of people that were round about them, and bowed themselves unto them, and provoked the Lord to anger.

> 13 And they forsook the Lord, and served Baal and Ashtaroth [Asherah].

After Joshua, Israel was ruled by a series of judges. "And it came to pass, when [each] judge was dead [and before a new one could be established], that they [the Israelites] returned, and corrupted themselves more than their fathers, in following other gods to serve them, and to bow down unto them; they ceased not from their own doings, nor from their stubborn way" (Judges 2:19). After Jair, the eighth judge, died almost two hundred years after Joshua, the Scriptures are more specific again in the Israelites' vacillating between serving the Lord and other gods about 1200 B.C.E.:

> And the children of Israel did evil again in the sight of the Lord, and served Baalim, and Ashtaroth [Asherah], and the gods of Syria, and the gods of

Zidon, and the gods of Moab, and the gods of the children of Ammon, and the gods of the Philistines, and forsook the Lord, and served not him. (Judges 10:6)

Although the Israelites served the gods of the Philistines, about two hundred years later war broke out between the Israelites and the Philistines. If the Israelites were to be successful, they could not continue serving the Philistines' gods, so Samuel addressed the people (I Samuel 7):

3 And Samuel spake unto all the house of Israel, saying, If ye do return unto the Lord with all your hearts, then put away the strange gods and Ashtaroth from among you, and prepare your hearts unto the Lord, and serve him only: and he will deliver you out of the hand of the Philistines.

4 Then the children of Israel did put away Baalim and Ashtaroth, and served the Lord only.

With the war against the Philistines still not settled, the people demanded that Samuel give them a king that can deliver them. So Saul was appointed king. But the Israelites apparently were vacillating again, for a few decades after the appeal in the previous paragraph, Samuel had to address them again, telling them of the many times Jehovah had delivered His people. They repented: "And they cried unto the Lord, and said, We have sinned, because we have forsaken the Lord, and have served Baalim and Ashtaroth: but now deliver us out of the hand of our enemies, and we will serve thee" (I Samuel 12:10).

Ironically, when a few years later Saul and his three sons were slain in battle with the Philistines, "they cut off his head, and stripped off his armour, and sent into the land of the Philistines round about, to publish it in the house of their idols, and among the people. And they put his armour in the house [temple] of Ashtaroth..." (I Samuel 31:9, 10).

Then David became king. He had already killed Goliath, the giant Philistine, and had proven himself on the battlefield. If not in all the countryside, at least in the courts of David, Jehovah was God.

After forty years, Solomon followed his father to the throne. For most of his life, he heeded his father David's example in being faithful to God, even building Jerusalem's first temple dedicated to Jehovah. But he loved and married many foreign women, including "the daughter of Pharaoh, women of the Moabities, Ammonites, Edomites, Zidonians, and Hittites" (I Kings 11:1), women all from arranged marriages from neighboring kingdoms so as to secure his borders. But

> 4 ...when Solomon was old,....his wives turned away his heart after other gods: and his heart was not perfect with the Lord his God, as was the heart of David his father.

> 5 For Solomon went after Ashtoreth [Asherah] the goddess of the Zidonians, and after Milcom the abomination of the Ammonites.

> 8 And likewise did he for all his strange [foreign] wives, which burnt incense and sacrificed unto their gods.

When Hezekiah became king of Judah thirteen sovereigns later, he removed the images from high places and broke them. He also broke "in pieces the brasen serpent that Moses had made [in the wilderness to cure those bitten by vipers in the desert exodus from Egypt]: for unto those days [Hezekiah's] the children of Israel did burn incense to it..." (II Kings 18:4) as though Moses' brazen serpent represented the serpent goddess Asherah herself.

The two kings between Hezekiah and Josiah the Yahwists considered the worst. That means for fifty-seven years the courts of Israel were again worshipping the serpent goddess, the Queen of Heaven, the protector of fertility and childbirth. Patai summarizes the return of Asherah, "Manasseh's act was the conviction that Yahweh's consort, the great mother-goddess Asherah, must be restored to her old and lawful place at the side of her husband."[9] But as Patai puts it, "With Joshiah (639-609 B.C.E.), another reformer came to the throne whose Yahwist zeal, stimulated by the discovery of the *Book of Deuteronomy* in the eighteenth year of his reign, surpassed even that of Hezekiah."[10] II Kings 23 reveals this zeal:

12 And the altars that were on the top of the upper chamber of Ahaz, which the kings of Judah had made, and the altars which Manasseh had made in the two courts of the house of the Lord, did the king beat down, and brake them down from thence, and cast the dust of them into the brook Kidron.

13 And the high places that were before Jerusalem, which were on the right hand of the mount of corruption, which Solomon the king of Israel had builded for Ashtoreth [Asherah] the abomination of the Zidonians, and for Chemosh the abomination of the Moabites, and for Milcom the abomination of the children of Ammon, did the king defile.

14 And he brake in pieces the images, and cut down the groves, and filled their places with the bones of men.

After Josiah, the religious pendulum, as one might expect by now, swung back to Asherah in the courts of the kingdom. It had always remained steady in the countryside in favor of the serpent goddess. Then about 587 or 586 B.C.E., King Nebuchadnezzar of Babylon destroyed Jerusalem and burned the temple. But Jeremiah escaped being carried off into Babylon and tried carrying on the Lord's work. While in Egypt, he tried to persuade the Jews there to forsake Asherah, whom they called the "queen of heaven," and return to Judah where they were needed. Their rejection of Jeremiah showed just how strong a hold Asherah had on these Jews (Jeremiah 44):

15 Then all the men which knew that their wives had burned incense unto other gods, and all the women that stood by, a great multitude, even all the people that dwelt in the land of Egypt, in Pathros, answered Jeremiah, saying,

16 As for the word that thou hast spoken unto us in the name of the Lord, we will not hearken unto thee.

17 But we will certainly do whatsoever thing goeth forth out of our own mouth, to burn incense unto the queen of heaven, and to pour out drink-offerings unto her, as we have done, we, and our fathers, our kings, and our princes, in the cities of Judah, and in the streets of Jerusalem: for then had we plenty of victuals, and were well, and saw no evil.

18 But since we left off to burn incense to the queen of heaven, and to pour out drink offerings unto her, we have wanted all things, and have been consumed by the sword and by the famine.

The women then apparently stepped up and said, if not already intermittently with the men, these words unto Jeremiah,

19 And when we burned incense to the queen of heaven, and poured out drink offerings unto her, did we make her cakes to worship her, and pour out drink offerings unto her, without our men?

The Jews who were carried off into Babylonian captivity apparently viewed their religious situation differently. They thought they were being punished for having burned incense to the queen of heaven. Archaeologists have found no evidence of the pregnant clay idols of Asherah amongst Hebrew ruins once the Jews had spent forty years in captivity and finally were allowed to return to Judah.[11]

Now that the Jews of Palestine were monotheistic, we should note, as we will soon more understandably see, it took more than guilt to persuade the Jewish women to give up Asherah and the promises she held out to Hebrew women seeking pregnancy and waiting apprehensively the birth. By this time, Jehovah had evolved into a masculine-feminine God, just as Elohim always was. The feminine element at that time was no longer disenfranchised from the Jewish Godhead.

# Elohim and Jehovah Contrasted

Now that we have covered the Hebrews' vacillating between the deities of matriarchy and patriarchy, let us examine next the two concepts of one God that rose up to combat the fertility goddess: Elohim and Jehovah. The nature of Elohim was fairly constant over the Old Testament millenniums. In contrast, that of Jehovah had moved 180 degrees, from an anthropomorphic male to an incorporeal male-female Being, and then after the Old Testament, back again among the Jews to about its original position minus the anthropomorphism.

In Genesis 1, the word translated as *God* is the plural noun *Elohim*. We learn the following about Elohim's image and likeness:

> 26 And God said, Let us make man in our image, after our likeness: ...

> 27 So God created man in his own image, in the image of God created he him; male and female created he them.

> 31 And God saw every thing that he had made, and, behold, it was very good.

Both males and females were created as "very good," both the image and likeness of God, Elohim, both equally innocent.

In Genesis 2, we have the other presentation of God in the Old Testament. In a mist that develops (vs 6), a more materialistic creation emerges. The term translated as *Lord God* is *Jehovah Elohim*. Pitted against the Lord God is the serpent, that ancient symbol of the ruling goddess during the matriarchic era millenniums before who had carried over as a fertility-goddess idol among Hebrew women into the patriarchic era until the idol was finally lost during the Babylonian captivity. The tree of life represented the worship of the one true God. The serpent wrapped itself around the tree of the knowledge of good and evil, a mixture of the worship of God and the material fertility idol. Because Eve would listen to the serpent, she must suffer for anything related to fertility—her menstruation, travailing, anything associated with birthing. Because Eve, representing woman, had listened to the idol's symbol and tempted Adam, the so-called pure image and

14

likeness, drawing him away from the tree of life to a knowledge of good and evil, she has condemned womanhood as demonic, deceptive, impure—a view of women that has lasted down through the ages and for most of Christendom. When Hebrew theologians used a story of a patriarchic Lord God to attack the very ancient but still current matriarchic fertility-goddess idol, patriarchy became more entrenched. Thus is the creation made in the allegorical mist.[12]

What a contrast between these two views of God and creation! In Genesis 1, Elohim has made both male and female *good*, both in His image and likeness. Beginning with Genesis 2:6, Jehovah has made both the tree of life *and* the tree of the knowledge of good and evil (vs 9), thus subtly giving the serpent a foothold, or should we say, a coilhold, in creation. Instead of everything being good as in the first chapter of Genesis, here a mixture of good and evil prevails, demoting man and condemning woman.

This distinction between Elohim and Jehovah and their respective creations continues through Genesis 13, after which the two terms and concepts are often used interchangeably, causing from time to time, as we shall see, some confusion and contradictions. Some believe that the name Lord God Jehovah is a *personal* name of Deity, but the term Elohim God is a *divine* Being. Mixing the personal with the divine may be a contributing factor in this confusion. In the meantime, the idea of womanhood is racketed about like a ball in a tennis match.

The personal name *Lord God* reflects the patriarchy of the times. For example, in Exodus 15:3 we read: "The Lord is a man of war: the Lord is his name." In contrast, the divine nature of Elohim, though intertwined with Jehovah's name, can be seen in Habakkuk 1:12, 13:

> 12 Art thou not from everlasting, O Lord my God, mine Holy One? we shall not die. O Lord, thou hast ordained them for judgment; and, O mighty God, thou hast established them for correction.

> 13 Thou art of purer eyes than to behold evil, and canst not look on iniquity: ...

In verse 12 above, "O Lord my God" carries the same meaning as *Lord God, Jehovah Elohim.* The "O Lord" refers to Jehovah. And

"O mighty God" is *Taûr*, or Rock, the mighty God. Since *Elohim* means "the Almighty," it would appear that *Taûr* is closer to Elohim than to Jehovah. In any case, the names for God in verse 12 are an intertwining of the Elohistic and Jehovistic terms, a mixture of the divine and personal.

The *nature* of this God, however, is seen in the beginning of verse 13. This is Elohim, the divine nature with "purer eyes than to behold evil," one who cannot "look on iniquity." In contrast, Jehovah in Genesis 2 beheld evil when creating the tree of the knowledge of good and evil. The divine, non-personal nature is neither matriarchic nor patriarchic. Neither the feminine nor the masculine nature dominates; they are equal in purity, without iniquity or sin.

Is testosterone more associated with the God Elohim of absolute Purity, or with the God Jehovah, who is a "man of war"? It is easy to spot the patriarchy, isn't it?

## How the Two Concepts of God Got Mixed Together

How did all this mixing of the personal and divine, the Jehovistic and Elohistic, take place?

To begin with, we read in Exodus (6:2, 3):

> 2 And God spake unto Moses, and said unto him, I am the Lord:
>
> 3 And I appeared unto Abraham, unto Isaac, and unto Jacob, by the name of God Almighty [*El Shaddai*, Hebrew for "God, the One of the Mountain(s)"], but by my name JEHOVAH was I not known to them.

According to Ussher's dates, Abraham, Isaac, and Jacob lived about 2,000 years after the biblical records of creation. About 500 years later, Moses is recorded to have introduced Jehovah to the Hebrews.[13] He probably picked up the name when he was exiled from Egypt and lived among the Midianites. There he married a daughter of Jethro, who was a priest of Midian and was believed to have worshipped Jehovah, a name for God among some non-Hebrew Semites. So if the story of Jehovah's creating Adam and throwing in Eve as a helpmate came about during the first 2,500 years of creation according to Ussher, then it evolved by non-Hebrews.[14]

Scholars tell us that the story of Adam and Eve, along with the first five books of the Bible, was first written as part of the Jehovistic record in the courts of David and/or his son Solomon or shortly thereafter.[15] That means that the story of Adam and Eve was written in scroll for the first time about or later than 3,000 years after it was supposed to have occurred. And according to James Hastings' *Dictionary of the Bible*, these scribes colored the first five books with the theological ideas of David's times.[16] Since one of the goals of Israel during David's reign was to rid Israel of all idols, including that of the fertility goddess prayed to by many Israelite women, the story of Adam and Eve could have been "colored" to accomplish that goal, as the story is described above.

Remember, when Solomon was old, his many foreign wives convinced him to worship many foreign gods (see I Kings 11). He even placed an idol of the serpent-goddess Asherah in Jehovah's temple. Remember how the Jewish women in Egypt convinced their men to worship Asherah, "the queen of heaven," and thus rejected Jeremiah's appeal to return to Jehovah. Before the Babylonian exile, the Yahwist scribes apparently had trouble competing with women who burnt incense to the serpent deity whom the women believed protected them in fertility and childbirth. Could Eve be symbolic of all these women as she too, according to the Jehovistic writers, listened to the serpent and was condemned to painful childbirth?

According to *A Standard Bible Dictionary*, "the name of J' [Jehovah] received an interpretation which released it from all mere physical association (Ex 3:13), made it the name of a supreme and living personality and attracted to itself the truth in older names (El, Elohim, El Shaddai [God Almighty], Adonai...)."[17] The scribes tried to base their personal God upon older ideas of a divine God.

Why even introduce a personal God? Scholars say that Moses did it because of the idolatry of his times. The enslaved Hebrews were bombarded by all kinds of gods while in Egypt, and these gods all had a personal name, an important concept in ancient times. Thus Moses knew that the people would be asking him for a personal name of the God that was to lead them out of Egypt. Millenniums later, after Baal and other gods no longer were tempting the Israelites, including the fertility goddess, who had not survived the Babylonian captivity, the personal God Jehovah gradually was being replaced by the divine God Elohim. Slowly, the name Jehovah, or as the Jews call Him, Jahweh (another spelling for Yahweh), began to be replaced as Jehovah's personal anthropomorphism faded until we find "the almost constant use of 'Elohim' rather than of 'Jahweh' in the later books of OT [Old Testament]."[18] But even with that development, both Jews and Christians constantly have gone back to Genesis 2 to revisit Jehovah and His son Adam and that sinner of sinners, Eve.

The Elohistic record of the first five books of the Bible was written in scroll about 150 years after the Jehovistic and is ascribed to one known only as the Elohist.[19] According to *The Interpreter's Bible*, "The great advance in the Elohist's thinking about God centers on the question of God's name, for he seems to have realized that a god had a personal name only when there were more gods than one. God has no personal name when he is God. He is the one that is: I AM."[20] And I might add, it was this Elohist who recorded Elohim's image and likeness as being both male and female. A complete God—with all the good qualities of masculinity and femininity— has a complete image and likeness reflected when this God looks into the mirror of infinity.

In the seventh century B.C.E., a third document surfaced called the "Deuteronomic." In the next century, an editor combined this new document with both the Jehovistic and Elohistic documents.[21] About this same time, a priestly individual compiled all the temple records that had been salvaged and taken into Babylonian captivity. While still in the Exile, another priestly figure then combined this new compilation with the previous compilation of the Jehovistic, Elohistic, and Deuteronomic, making a new intertwined and mixed document from the four.[22] The personal and the divine, the Jehovistic and Elohistic understandings of Deity, were confusing combination resulting in the Pentateuch. Confusing because is God all masculine or both masculine and feminine? Confusing because is God's image the all masculine Adam of Jehovah, or both the male and female of Elohim?

Let us examine a few passages, some where there is clarity and some not so clear. The more ideas were combined, the harder it is to find the true nature of the image and likeness in the theological combinations. Some passages remain intact, beautiful, even poetic and inspiring, but the greater portion dealing with the nature of the image and likeness and of womanhood become quite confusing. One metaphors [comes to mind: separating the wheat from the chaff that will require some thoughtful examination.

# Anthropomorphic Jehovah Becomes Both Male and Female

We'll start with Jehovah. He began as an all-male God, "man of war," mighty warrior, standing against the goddess of matriarchy. When the women of the general Hebrew population refused to deny Asherah as the goddess of fertility and childhood, we find passages coincidently representing Jehovah as both male and female Himself. This appeared to counteract the belief in popular religion that the all-male Jehovah was married to the goddess Asherah. However, the male anthropomorphisms and the female anthropomorphisms combined into one Supreme Being would get a bit awkward, to say the least. Imagine, as we shall see in our first example: God, a mighty warrior, with a womb.

The passage is from the Book of Job (38:1, 22, 23, 28, 29):

> 1 Then the Lord answered Job out of the whirlwind, and said,

> 22 Hast thou entered into the treasures of the snow? or hast thou seen the treasures of the hail,

> 23 Which I have reserved against the time of trouble, against the day of battle and war?

> 28 Hath the rain a father? or who hath begotten the drops of dew?

> 29 Out of whose womb came the ice? and the hoary frost of heaven, who hath gendered it?

The name of the *Lord* and the reference to "the day of battle and war" show that we are dealing with Jehovah. But note that the creator of the universe is called both father and mother (because of that created from the womb of God).

A second passage combining both the male and female anthropomorphisms in Jehovah is in the Book of Isaiah (42:13, 14). These verses deal with the Hebrews in Exile in Babylon. The passage appears in a section where its author is chastening the Israelites for their past sins. Apparently, Judah has not yet let go of the goddess Asherah. This passage falls into what biblical scholars

19

call Second Isaiah. *Harper's Bible Dictionary* says, "The author of Second Isaiah sought to change his audience's religious attitude."[23] In this passage (see below), the Lord Jehovah is not only a mighty warrior but also one whose womb is ready to deliver. He counters Asherah as the Deity of fertility and childbirth.

> 13 The Lord shall go forth as a mighty man, he shall stir up jealousy like a man of war: he shall cry, yea, roar; he shall prevail against his enemies.

> 14 I have long time holden my peace; I have been still, and refrained myself: now will I cry like a travailing woman; I will destroy and devour at once.

The whole tone of verse 13 pictures Jehovah as "a mighty man," "a man of war." This same tone also saturates the following verse. The roaring like "a travailing woman" brings to mind the ancient stories of those fierce Amazon women, who could rise immediately after giving birth and ride forth into battle with one breast cut off so as not to interfere with shooting their bows. In context, Isaiah apparently saw Jehovah fighting those who worshipped "graven images" (42:17) and giving birth to a better, idolatry-free Israel.

But let's take another look at the last clause of verse 14: "I will destroy and devour at once." The Hebrew word translated *destroy* is *nasham*, whose root, according to Strong's, means "to *blow* away." And the Hebrew word translated *devour* is *sha'aph*, whose root means "to *inhale* eagerly" and can be translated *pant*. The Douay Bible renders this clause similarly to that in the King James: "I will destroy, and swallow up at once." But the Revised Standard Version reads, "I will gasp and pant"; the Modern Reader's Bible, "I will gasp and pant together"; the New English Bible (Oxford Study Edition), simply "whimpering, panting and gasping"; and Moffatt's Bible, simply "panting and gasping."

Doesn't "I will gasp and pant" following "now will I cry like a travailing woman" better fit the simile of a woman giving birth than the words "I will destroy and devour at once"? The focus switches from destroying to birthing, giving birth to a new Israel. A lot less testosterone, more estrogen. What a change in the imagery! Perhaps the male translators back in the 1600s (those of the King James and Douay versions) had heard a travailing woman cry out or scream in the next room but were not aware of all the gasping and panting. By the time we have the newer translations in the 1900s, apparently the word had gotten out. Of course men today who have been through a Lamaz course and have held the hand of the woman who is about to make them a father know all about the gasping and panting. I wonder whether Isaiah had had an equivalent course to Lamaz some 2,700 years ago. Probably not, but somehow he was familiar with the process. In any case, we get a clearer picture of Jehovah as both male and female.

Some say that the above passage only appears to represent Jehovah as both masculine and feminine because of the mistranslation in the King James and Douay versions of the "gasping and panting" while a woman is in travail. In actuality, they hold, we have the masculine Jehovah as the "mighty man" and "man of war," on the one hand, and the feminine portion of Elohim as Mother, on the other hand. In other words, a mixture of the natures of Jehovah and Elohim.[24] In any case, it raises the confusing question, how can a man of war also be a travailing mother? Is this a case of a mixed metaphor? We can see both masculine and feminine natures in Elohim, but at the metaphorical or anthropomorphic level, the image of a mighty man gasping and panting in childbirth, stretches the imagination. The one thing it does do is paint God as Mother as well as Father and should open the understanding about females also as the image and likeness of God.

Let's look at another passage from Isaiah (66:9): "Shall I bring to the birth, and not cause to bring forth? saith the Lord." This passage appears in the second portion or chief division of the Book of Isaiah, looking here beyond the Babylonian captivity. As said before, by this time Jehovah was taking on a feminine nature as well as masculine. This Asherah promise of fertility harmony was now being transferred to Jehovah's newly feminine nature.

## Non-anthropomorphic Elohim Both Masculine and Feminine

Next we move to the Elohistic tradition. As said before, Elohim has been cited as being both masculine and feminine because in Genesis 1 Elohim's likeness is both male and female, just like the image's creator. There is no need for anthropomorphisms of either gender to make the case. The human is not needed to present the divine.

21

# Exception: Male-Female El Shaddai in the Elohim Tradition Uses Anthropomorphisms

One of the other older names for God in the Elohistic tradition, *El Shaddai*, is different. No anthropomorphism has been needed to present the maleness of *the Almighty*. But what about Shaddai's female side?

Jehovah has already been shown to have a womb and has experienced travailing. Now with Shaddai we add breasts to accompany the womb, a God with breasts. The passage to examine is Genesis 49:25:

> Even by the God [Elohim] of thy father, who shall help thee; and by the Almighty [Shaddai], who shall bless thee with blessings of heaven above, blessings of the deep that lieth under, blessings of the breasts, and of the womb.

In Hebrew, instead of repeating the same term for God in two consecutive clauses, the writer would use what he considered equivalent names for God. Therefore, this passage would suggest that Shaddai is part of the Elohistic tradition.

Cutting through the verbiage of the passage above, we have "the Almighty...shall bless thee with...blessings of the breasts, and of the womb." *Shaddai*, usually translated as *the Almighty* in English, according to some biblical scholars, means "the God with Breasts."[25] Other scholars also say that *the Almighty* is not the best translation; they prefer "the Mountain(s),"[26] which may help explain "the God with Breasts," for sometimes the natural silhouette of mountains may appear as breasts, like the Bubbles at the end of Jordan Pond in Acadia National Park on Mount Dessert Island, Maine, or the distant mountains viewed over the fjords as seen from Spitsbergen, Norway. In any case, the imagery is one of the Hebrew God as female. With a womb, travailing, and breasts for nursing, this God Shaddai is Mother. With Almightiness and strength, the God Shaddai is also Father. The Father-Mother God, one complete Supreme Being with two natures. Not an all-male God, as Jehovah sometimes was described, married to the goddess Asherah in the popular religion. We are right back to Elohim with a male-female image and likeness.

# El Shaddai's Anthropomorphisms Fade Over Time

Let's examine another verse, this one from Job 33:4: "The Spirit of God [El] hath made me, and the breath of the Almighty [Shaddai] hath given me life."

Remember, in Hebrew, when two terms for God are used in consecutive clauses, the terms are considered synonymous. The words *breath* and *given me life* suggest the Motherhood of Shaddai. El has always been acknowledged as masculine, and in popular religion, as stated earlier in this present chapter, was thought to be married to Asherah and to be father of the god Baal. Here El, whose name is adopted by the Hebrews as the one God, appears as Father and Shaddai as Mother, not two married Beings, but again as one Father-Mother God with two natures. And what stands out this time, although the name *Shaddai* suggests breasts, God's Motherhood does not require any direct mentioning of female anthropomorphisms (motherly body parts) to identify Her. Since this verse in Job is dealing with the creation of God's image and likeness, like Elohim's children in Genesis 1, the image must be the same as the creator, both male and female.

The name *El Shaddai* was very popular in the first five books of the Bible. Outside those books it appears about three dozen times in Scripture with 83% of these found in the Book of Job. William Smith writes that "throughout Job the name Shaddai stands in parallelism with Elohim, and never with Jehovah."[27] This verifies that the image and likeness being created in Job 33:4 is *not* Jehovah's Adamic sinner.

# Masculine-Feminine Jehovah's Anthropomorphisms Also Fade

In the passages discussed before of *Jehovah's* Motherhood, anthropomorphism was used to make the point. In the following two passages Jehovah's Motherhood is revealed without any anthropomorphism.

First, the idea of God as Mother is probably more suggestive in Isaiah 66:13: "As one whom his mother comforteth, so will I comfort you..." A human mother has breasts and a womb and has gone through travailing. If God metaphorically has breasts and a womb and has experienced travailing, gasping and panting, then this human idea of God certainly is Mother. Here in the last chapter of Isaiah, however, when the Jews exiled in Babylon had repented and were looking for comfort, the focus is less on the physical and more on the comforting nature of a mother, a mother's love. "As with a human mother, so with the divine Mother" appears to be the lesson here.

Second, the Mother-love theme was unveiled back in Deuteronomy 32. Verse 4 appears to be in the Elohistic tradition of El's being without iniquity when we know that Jehovah in Genesis 2 is accredited with not only knowing evil but also creating it. Next, down in Verses 11 and 12 we have the Jehovistic tradition, but with God's appearing as a mother eagle without any human anthropomorphism. The message here is that, when we worship only the one God, Jehovah protects us as a mother would. Lastly, in verse 18 we are back to the Elohistic views:

> 4 He is the Rock, his work is perfect: for all his ways are judgment: a God [El] of truth and without iniquity, just and right is he.

> 11 As an eagle stirreth up her nest, fluttereth over her young, spreadeth abroad her wings, taketh them, beareth them on her wings:

> 12 So the Lord [Jehovah] alone did lead him, and there was no strange god [such as Asherah or her son Baal] with him.

> 18 Of the Rock that begat thee thou art unmindful, and hast forgotten God [El] that formed thee.

In both verses 4 and 18 God is El, who is treated synonymously with "the Rock." Is "the Rock" comparable to Shaddai, God of the Mountain(s)? *The Interpreter's Dictionary of the Bible* recognizes the possibility of such a relationship.[28] In any case, since verse 4, as explained above, appears to be in the Elohistic tradition, verse 18, by way of association, appears to be Elohistic likewise.

Furthermore, in verse 18, the word translated *begat* and often associated with the male, also, according to Strong's, can be translated *bore, birthed, brought forth (children, young), travailed.* Thus, *begat* can be a feminine function or a masculine one, or both in the case of the Rock. In other words, the Rock is both masculine and feminine at the same time. Where it says, "God that formed thee," *formed*, according to Strong's, can be translated *brought forth, travailed (with pain)*. Again, God is presented as both masculine and feminine, and it would appear to be an arrogant and/or patriarchic thought that would skip over the feminine.

## Feminine Racham: Mercy

Both the Elohistic and Jehovistic traditions used a certain Hebrew word translated *mercy* in order to appeal to the feminine side of the creator for compassion. Different Hebrew words are translated *mercy* but let us examine two passages where the rare use of *racham* is so translated. According to Strong's, *racham* means *compassion* and can be translated also as *damsel, tender love, (great, tender) mercy, womb* ("as *cherishing* the foetus"). The implication is that the source of such mercy is feminine.

The first example is found in Genesis 43:14. In this verse, the God Almighty is El. The fifteen references to God before this verse all are Elohim, with most before that also Elohim. The nine after it also refer to Elohim, with most after that also Elohim. According to Exodus 6:3, Jacob never knew God as Jehovah. Thus the passage would appear to fit into the Elohistic tradition.

Here, Jacob, now renamed Israel, tells his son Judah to go back to Egypt to buy more food for the family during the famine and hopefully bring back one of Judah's brothers who was being held hostage until their return to Egypt. Israel offers this prayer, "And God Almighty give you mercy before the man." Those who know the story know that "the man" here is Joseph, whom Judah and his other brothers had sold into Egyptian slavery. In this prayer, Israel appealed to the feminine side of God Almighty for great, tender mercy to restore his family and bring home food.

The other example with the rare use of *racham* translated as *mercy* appears at the end of Nehemiah's prayer that Artaxerxes the king will allow Nehemiah, in Babylonian captivity, to return to Jerusalem to restore the walls and establish there some civil authority (Nehemiah 1:11):

> O Lord, I beseech thee, let now thine ear be attentive
> to the prayer of thy servant, and to the prayer of
> thy servants, who desire to fear [also translated,

*to revere*] thy name: and prosper, I pray thee, thy servant this day, and grant him mercy in the sight of this man.

Often the word *Lord* is translated from *Jehovah*, but here Nehemiah in "O Lord" used the word *Adonai*, which simply means *Lord* when referring to God. Since some Jews won't pronounce the name of Yahweh out of respect for their God but say Adonai, an older term for God, instead and since Nehemiah was Jewish, this passage is probably part of the Jehovistic tradition.[29] Recognizing Jehovah as also feminine was typical near the end of the Exile. In any case, he is appealing to the feminine side of God for great, tender mercy, for the compassion a mother would have for a cherished child in her womb.

## Jehovah Joins Elohim as Being Both Masculine and Feminine

As Dr. Patai points out, "...contrary to the generally held view, the religion of the Hebrews and the Jews was never without at least a hint of the feminine in its God-concept."[30] At first, the goddess Asherah was thought, at least in popular religion, to be married to the ancient Canaanite god, El. Later, her husband was Jehovah Himself. In the beginning of the official record called the Scriptures, Jehovah appeared more like a masculine, mental idol disguised in anthropomorphisms. Elohim, El Shaddai, was already established as the masculine-feminine God with a masculine declension (grammatical word ending) to His name, who had made man in His image, both male and female. With time, Jehovah was described as both masculine and feminine. Patai writes, "Following the destruction of the First Temple [586 B.C.E.], the idea slowly gained ground that the one and only God comprised two aspects, a male and a female one, and the Cherubim [one male and one female] in the Holy of Holies of the Second Temple were the symbolic representation of these two divine virtues or powers."[31]

This brings us to the end of the Old Testament. With idolatry gone since the return from Exile, with persecution down to virtually nothing, the two main ingredients for needing a personal God, such as the Hebrew Jehovah birthed during the Egyptian slavery, were now withdrawn from the recipe for Deity. With anthropomorphisms having been gone for at least a century—both physical features and human personality vanquished—Jehovah and Elohim had become basically the same male-female God.

## The Concept of Jehovah After the Old Testament

What happened to the Jewish God after the close of the Hebrew Scriptures? During the 400 years between the prophets and the Christian Messiah, foreign powers forced idolatry on the Jews, even placing an idol of Jupiter in the Jerusalem Temple. Persecutions returned and continued for millenniums, to beyond World War II. The two ingredients for desiring a personal God had returned. Another change in their Deity should therefore be expected. Patai summarizes what happened: At times, as during the 800 years from the second century B.C.E. through the sixth century C.E. and even more so afterwards, "the female element in the deity was effectively pushed into the background." At other times, as during the biblical period and what is called the Kabbalistic era, that is, when Jews also used a set of scriptures outside of what Christians call the Old Testament, the female concept or portion of God "occupied an important place in popular theology, occasionally even to the extent of overshadowing the male deity or the male component of the godhead. Only in the most recent times, after the Kabbalistic upsurge had subsided" and the Hasidic teachings of some Orthodox Jews in a small section of Europe during the mid-eighteenth century receded, "was the female element eliminated from the God-concept among Reform, Conservative, and non-Hasidic Orthodox Jews, leaving it centered upon a strictly spiritual, but nevertheless inescapably masculine Godhead, upon 'our Father in heaven.'"[32]

Today, Jewish women have more rights in the United States and western European countries than in the past. I attended a Jewish service in Vermont ten years ago in which the women were allowed to sit anywhere with the men and the guest speaker was a biblical scholar and professor, a woman. Afterwards, the rabbi greeted my wife and me, gentile Christians, with a handshake of love. As of this writing, conservative-oriented New Hampshire has at least two female rabbis. Nationally, since 1972 when the first woman was ordained a rabbi, more than 350 other women have been ordained rabbis of various branches of American Judaism.[33]

In Israel itself, women do not have as much religious freedom because the government is controlled by Orthodox Judaism, which will not ordain a woman. In an interview with Rabbi Naamah Kelman, Israel's first woman rabbi (outside of Orthodoxy, of course), Len Ly reports in March 2010 that "if an Israeli wants her marriage recognized in Israel, but does not want to be wed by an Orthodox rabbi, she needs to leave Israel for the ceremony. When she returns, the marriage will be recognized under international law."[34] Sheera Frenkel reports in United States newspapers in the summer of 2010 that in Israel, when women go to the Wailing Wall to pray, they sometimes are harassed. "Orthodox men and women have spit at, cursed and attacked" these women. Then the Israeli police come and arrest these praying women "on charges of disturbing the peace." One woman was even arrested at the Wailing Wall for praying from the Torah.[35]

Although some Jewish sects understand Jehovah to be both male and female, most Christians agree with the Orthodox Jews in believing that He is all male. Christians, who often focus on the New Testament more than the Old, have mistakenly considered Jehovah as stable as the male-female Elohim, that a personal God does not change but stays the same as does a divine God. However, a personal God like Jehovah changes with the people's idea of Deity.


## Conclusion

In summary, Jehovah started out as an all-male Being, anthropomorphic as a "man of war" with physical strength and varying human personalities. With the early Hebrews' and later just the Jewish popular religion's painting a picture of Jehovah married to the goddess Asherah, Jehovah evolved into a male-female God, one God with two aspects instead of a male God married to a female entity. Jehovah was given Asherah's power of overseeing fertility and childbirth. When idolatry was eliminated and persecution controlled, Jehovah's anthropomorphism evaporated, and the personal Jehovah for the first and only short period of about two hundred years was similar to the divine, male-female Elohim. At that point the Old Testament ends, for the first time essentially having one concept of the Supreme Being.

Then the Jews had idolatry forced on them and persecution returned for over two millenniums. Consequently, the personal God Jehovah changed again, still leaving the anthropomorphism in the past, but limiting His scope of qualities for much of Judaism to an all-male Deity.

Not recognizing the change factor in a personal Jehovah leaves Christians adopting the Adam and Eve story without question, a story written more than 3,000 years after it was supposed to have happened, a story painting Eve as Hebrews' womanhood listening to the serpent-goddess Asherah instead of to the all-male Jehovah, a story about Hebrew womanhood's punishment for turning to the fertility and childhood goddess instead of to the all-male, dominate Deity. We must remember that women had lost almost all their rights and privileges to patriarchic superstitions about women's menstrual cycles. Patriarchy was subordinating women, women who were looking for help in the remnants of matriarchy. Because women were looking to the feminine for help, they were to be chastised. Because Hebrew men chose to focus on an all-male Jehovah instead of the male-female Elohim who made man in His image, both male and female, the women had to be subordinated and punished with guilt until they submitted.

Today school children study the work of Marie Curie, more known as Madame Curie, the famous scientist about a hundred years ago, recipient of two Nobel Prizes. She is now much more recognized in history than her husband. Yet in 1903 when both she and her husband were awarded the first of her two Nobel Prizes, the president of the Swedish Academy noted at the awards ceremony his thought of her place by quoting the Bible: "It is not good that the man should be alone; I will make him an help meet for him." What an insult to this brilliant woman!

Then in 1910, just months before she was awarded her second Nobel Prize, she was snubbed again, this time by the male scientists of France by denying her membership in the French Academy. One Academy member claimed that "women cannot be part of the Institute of France."[36]

Are Christians going to focus on a continued subordination of women under an all-male Jehovah whose image and likeness is Adam, with the Eves of the world as helpmates to serve their Adams? Or should Christians focus on a male-female Elohim whose image and likeness includes both male and female? Would a divine God reduce the feminine half of humanity to bowing to the masculine? Has Jehovah, "the man of war" at the time of Genesis 2's story of creation, now called "the man upstairs," proven that testosterone has made the world more peaceful? Can an infinite, eternal Supreme Being express only half of the infinite array of qualities? Should human patriarchy dictate for humanity a limited nature of Deity and, on that basis, the plight of women?

Male-Female Elohim, or All-Male Jehovah? That is the question.
Minority-based Male-Female Jehovah, or All-Male Jehovah? That is the question.
Epicenarchy,[37] or Patriarchy? That is the question.

> To be, or not to be: that is the question:
> Whether 'tis nobler in the mind to suffer
> The slings and arrows of outrageous fortune,
> Or to take arms against a sea of troubles,
> And by opposing end them? ...

Shakespeare
*Hamlet*, Act 3, Scene 1

The Hebrews in Babylonian Exile worked vigorously to rid themselves of the snake and fertility goddess carved in wood, stone, and bone and made of clay. For the Hebrews, the triumph over physical idols was a victory for monotheism. Now the challenge is to determine and recognize the *true nature* of the one Mind of the universe. And of the image and likeness of this infinite God.

# Endnotes
## Chapter 2

1   Raphael Patai, *The Hebrew Goddess*, 3rd enlarged ed., Detroit: Wayne State University Press, 1978, pp. 54, 55.

2   Merlin Stone, *When God Was a Woman*, New York: Barnes & Noble, 1993, pp. 199, 201, 204, 205, 209, 210.
Patai, p. 58.

3   Patai, pp. 58, 59.

4   Patai, p. 58.

5   See note by C. I. Scofield, *The Scofield Reference Bible*, new and improved ed., New York: Oxford University Press, 1917, p. 289.
Stone, p. 9.

6   *Ibid.*
According to Ussher's dates, Abraham arrived in Canaan two to three thousand years after archaeological evidence that patriarchy had begun to replace matriarchy. So we must not conclude that Abraham had introduced patriarchy to the region.

7   Patai, p. 53. See also p. 49.

8   The Hebrews have not been the only ones trying to convert a people who believed in a fertility goddess to an all-male monotheism. Isabella and Ferdinand of Spain sent waves and waves of missionaries to the Americas to convert indigenous Americans to Catholicism. But the native Americans would not give up their fertility goddess. Eventually, there became a "marriage" between Catholicism and whatever fertility goddess existed in the local region, as evidenced, for example, from the Cerro del Tepeyac of Our Lady of Guadalupe in Mexico. The paintings of Our Lady of Guadalupe look like the Virgin Mary with an indigenous American face. Today, it is difficult to tell where the fusing of the religions begins and ends. See PBS's DVD *When Worlds Collide: The Untold Story of the Americas after Columbus*.

9   Patai, p. 49.

10  *Ibid.*

11  PBS's *NOVA* DVD, *The Bible's Buried Secrets: Beyond Fact or Fiction*, 2009.

12  See Stone's research in her Chapter 10 for more on Adam and Eve and the serpent.

13 James Hastings, *et al.*, *Dictionary of the Bible*, New York: Charles Scribner's Sons, 1937, p. 300.

14 A passage from Genesis 15:6 has God telling Abraham that by His name Jehovah did God bring Abraham out of Ur: "And he [God] said unto him, I am the LORD that brought thee out of Ur of the Chaldees..." About the time of Abraham's arrival, Genesis starts to use Elohim and Jehovah interchangeably. As we shall see, the Scriptures first began to be written down about a thousand years later in the courts of King David or shortly thereafter. After several versions came about—some favoring Elohim and others Jehovah—some other scribes combined the various writings into one to show that the Hebrew God was one Being. The intertwining may have taken place either during this combining of different versions of events or during the period of oral traditions where storytelling was passed down orally from generation to generation or perhaps during both processes. In any case, contradictions inevitably emerged, but they do not change the fact here that the story of Adam and Eve was supposed to have evolved at least two millenniums before the Hebrews were in the region and three before the story was recorded on scroll.

Another example of this confusing mixing of events pertaining to Elohim and Jehovah can be found in Genesis 5:1, 2 where the two stories of creation, that of Elohim and His likeness' being both male and female and that of Jehovah and His likeness being Adam, are intermixed as one story.

15 *The Interpreter's Dictionary of the Bible*, vol. I of V, Nashville: Abingdon Press, 1962, p. 860.

16 James Hastings, p. 299.

17 Melancthon W. Jacobus, *et al.*, *A Standard Bible Dictionary*, New York: Funk & Wagnalls Co., 1909, p. 297.

18 Hastings, p. 301.

19 *The Interpreter's Dictionary of the Bible*, vol. I, p. 860.

20 *The Interpreter's Bible*, vol. I of XII, New York: Abingdon-Cokesbury Press, 1952, p. 867.

21 *The Interpreter's Dictionary of the Bible*, vol. I, p. 860.

22 *Ibid.*, pp. 860-861.

23 *Harper's Bible Dictionary*, San Francisco: Harper & Row, 1985, p. 431.

24 Philo Judaeus (about 20 B.C.E.-54 C.E.), Jewish Hellenistic philosopher, also saw God as a mixture of gender natures, but

he thought Elohim was the masculine and Yahweh (Jehovah), the feminine. He is known for his negative views of women.

25  Virginia Ramey Mollenkott, *The Divine Feminine: The Biblical Imagery of God as Female*, New York: Crossroad, 1983, pp. 57, 58. (See this theology professor's book also for other feminine references to God that I have not covered.)

Phyllis Trible, "God, Nature of, in the Old Testament," *The Interpreter's Dictionary of the Bible*, Supplementary vol., p. 368. (The Hebrew writers liked to use paraonomasia, or wordplay, to connect and expand ideas. Here we have the Almighty (Shaddai) with breasts (shadayim). Since the two Hebrew words are spelled so similarly, the wordplay expands the definition of *Shaddai* itself to mean "the God with Breasts.")

26  For example, see Hastings, p. 299; and *The Interpreter's Dictionary of the Bible*, vol. 2, p. 412 and vol. 4, p. 301.

27  William Smith, *A Dictionary of the Bible*, Hartford: S. S. Scranton, 1868, p. 872.

28  *The Interpreter's Dictionary of the Bible*, vol. II, p. 415.

29  When the English first started translating Hebrew into English, they did not know the vowels for *YHWH*. They did not know that it was to be pronounced *Yahweh* because the Jews never said His name aloud but instead called Him *Adonai*. So the English took the three vowel sounds of *Adonai* and inserted them into *YHWH*, coming up with *Yehowah*, a three-syllable word instead of the two-syllable *Yahweh*. The changing of the *Y* to a *J* was probably a Latin influence, *Y* to *I* to *J*. Changing the *w* to *v* was probably the result of the British simplification of sounds. In any case, the name *Jehovah* came into English in 1518.

30  Patai, p. 279.

31  Patai, pp. 94-95.

32  Patai, p. 279.

33  *Jewish Women Encyclopedia*: http://jwa.org/encyclopedia/article/rabbis-in-united-states.

34  http://www.neontommy.com/2010/03/israelis-first-woman-rabbi-refl

35  Sheera Fenkel, McClatchy Newspapers, August 28, 2010.

36  See Julie Des Jardins, "The Passion of Madame Curie," *Smithsonian.Com*, October 2011, pp. 82-90.

37  Gender-neutral rule

# CHAPTER 3

## THREE MAJOR VIEWS OF WOMEN: JESUS, PLATO, AND ARISTOTLE

In this chapter, we will examine three different views of women—those of Jesus, those of Plato, and those of Aristotle. One might think that those of Christ Jesus would have had the largest influence on Western Christianity, but in fact those of Plato and especially Aristotle are in charge of Christianity's theology regarding women and thus most of Western culture's ideas of women. Such is the influence of ancient Greek philosophy. "How can this be?" one may ask. By the time readers finish this chapter, they should know exactly how it happened.

### Jesus' Views of Women

Jesus was born about five to seven years before the date calculated in ancient times and died on the cross about thirty years into the new common era. We don't know much about his boyhood except for the biblical story of his parents' finding him in deep conversation with the rabbis in Jerusalem. From that and the events later in his life, we can deduce that he was intelligent and well versed in the Hebrew Scriptures. His followers saw him as the prophesied Messiah. He is accredited with many parables and spiritual healings. Writers have described some of his acts as miracles because they cannot be explained. Others say that they were not miracles but instead the natural outcome of divine law as opposed to physical law. The climax of his life came when he arose from the dead, seen first by Mary Magdalene and then his doubting disciples, and finally ascended from this world.

The following passages and stories are from the Gospels, accompanied with some explanations and/or questions to consider.

1.  When Jesus was finishing his conversation with the woman of Samaria at Jacob's well, his disciples returned from buying supplies in the city "and marvelled that he talked with the woman" (John 4:27). J. R. Dummelow in his commentary on the Bible has this to say about Jesus' talking with the woman:

    In his high estimate of womanhood Jesus rose far above the ideas of his time, and taught lessons which are only now being learned (see on Mt 1:18-25). The contemporary rabbis refused to teach religion to women, and would not even speak to a woman in a public place.[1]

    The Gospels record how men of stature had asked Jesus to tell them plainly whether or not he was the prophesied Messiah (John 10:23-25), but Jesus would not. Yet he did tell this Samarian woman who had had five husbands and was then living with a man who was not her husband: "I that speak unto thee am he" (John 4:25, 26). Furthermore, he taught her the very nature of God: "God is a Spirit: and they that worship him must worship him in spirit and in truth" (John 4:24). No wonder why his disciples, conditioned by the patriarchy of their times, "marvelled that he talked with the woman."

2.  The Gospels also have other stories of Jesus' interacting with women. For example, in the following one, Jesus not only was teaching Mary but also admonished her sister Martha for being more concerned about the traditional "woman's work" instead of the word of Christ:

    38 ...a certain woman named Martha received him [Jesus] into her house.

    39 And she had a sister called Mary, which also sat at Jesus' feet, and heard his word.

40 But Martha was cumbered about much serving, and came to him, and said, Lord, dost thou not care that my sister hath left me to serve alone? bid her therefore that she help me.

41 And Jesus answered and said unto her, Martha, Martha, thou art careful and troubled about many things:

42 But one thing is needful: and Mary hath chosen that good part, which shall not be taken away from her. (Luke 10)

3. In John, we learn that "Now Jesus loved Martha, and her sister, and Lazarus" (11:5). A few verses further on we see Jesus teaching Martha about the resurrection:

21 Then said Martha unto Jesus, Lord, if thou hadst been here, my brother had not died.

22 But I know, that even now, whatsoever thou wilt ask of God, God will give it thee.

23 Jesus saith unto her, Thy brother shall rise again.

24 Martha saith unto him, I know that he shall rise again in the resurrection at the last day.

25 Jesus said unto her, I am the resurrection, and the life: he that believeth in me, though he were dead, yet shall he live:

26 And whosoever liveth and believeth in me shall never die. Believest thou this?

27 She saith unto him, Yea, Lord: I believe that thou art the Christ, the Son of God, which should come into the world.

28 And when she had so said, she went her way, and called Mary her sister secretly, saying, The Master is come, and calleth for thee.

4. Note in the next passage that, when Jesus travelled about the hillsides preaching, many women of means accompanied him and his disciples:

1 And it came to pass afterword, that he went throughout every city and village, preaching and shewing the glad tidings of the kingdom of God: and the twelve were with him,

2 And certain women, which had been healed of evil spirits and infirmities, Mary called Magdalene, out of whom went seven devils,

3 and Joanna the wife of Chuza Herod's steward, and Susanna, and many others, which ministered unto him of their substance.
(Luke 8)

Based upon Jesus' lecture to Martha cited above, that listening to the word of Christ was more important than doing traditional women's work, cannot one see these women not only ministering unto him but also sitting with his disciples around Jesus, soaking in every lesson on eternal life? Since three women were named and it was said there were "many others," could there have been about as many women as male disciples travelling with Jesus and receiving his preaching? Is this a point often overlooked?

5. Roman and Greek law in Jesus' time allowed women to divorce men as well as men to divorce women. But with Hebrews, the law of divorce was based upon the second chapter of Genesis where a man, made in the image of the anthropomorphic Lord God Jehovah, was regarded as superior to his helpmate, the female. In Hebrew law, a man could "write a bill of divorcement" in which he repudiated the woman and thus was immediately free of her. Such bills of divorcement were still used until at least the eleventh century of the common era among Jews.[2] The Pharisees

knew that there were two schools of thought on divorce among the Jews, one conservative view in which divorce could be granted only if the woman had committed adultery and the other a more loose view that allowed the man to divorce for any reason. So the Pharisees in Mark 10:2-9, trying to find cause to prosecute Jesus, tempted him, asking, "Is it lawful for a man to put away his wife?" Jesus avoided the controversy by quoting the Scriptures and advocating no divorce. The most interesting verses for our discussion here are 6 through 8 where Jesus was speaking:

6 But from the beginning of the creation God made them male and female.

7 For this cause shall a man leave his father and mother, and cleave to his wife;

8 And they twain shall be one flesh: so then they are no more twain, but one flesh.

Two points stand out here. First, Jesus referenced the first chapter of Genesis in which Elohim made His image and likeness both male and female. In contrast, the Pharisees, as already stated, were thinking in terms of the second chapter of Genesis in which the Lord God Jehovah had made a male human in His image and as a secondary thought shuffled in a disposable female helpmate. Jesus tried to raise the Pharisees' thought above the idea that women were simple objects for repudiation in a bill of divorcement.

Second, since the Pharisees' focus was on the second chapter of Genesis, Jesus quoted Genesis 2:24 where the two in marriage become one flesh. But with his previous quote on equality, the "one flesh" is one unit, one-to-one in one. The woman was not to be torn away from this unit as though she were some kind of disposable nonentity. Unlike the familiar dominant male and helpmate in Genesis 2, the two in Jesus' explanation were equals in Genesis 1. Despite the support from the old Scriptures, this idea was revolutionary in Jesus' day. No wonder women loved Jesus! He was indeed their Messiah!

6. In Matthew 6:9, we find the first line of the Lord's Prayer: "Our Father which art in heaven." Tertullian (160?-230?), an early father of the Latin church, wrote in his "On Prayer" his analysis of the Lord's Prayer. In his short chapter 2, he wrote that "in the Father and Son is recognized the mother, from whom arises the name both of Father and of Son."[3] The capitalization of *Father* and *Son* is supplied by the translator according to English custom; in Tertullian's original Latin, *patre*, *filio*, and *mater* are all equally uncapitalized. In saying "in the father and the son is recognized the mother," Tertullian was recognizing that without a mother, there can be no father, and vice versa. Therefore, God is both Father and Mother at the same time. But just as interesting is his next part of that clause in which he wrote that it is from the Mother that "arises the name both of Father and of Son." Although God, by definition, cannot be Mother without also being Father, and vice versa, the concept of God as Mother, he wrote, brought forth God's name as Father and revealed the Son. Just what point he was making here isn't completely clear unless he was thinking that when the Supreme Being as Mother bore the Son, the Supreme Being was then also Father, or it was to emphasize the Motherhood/Fatherhood of God.

Although Tertullian described God as both Mother and Father, an idea close to that of Elohim in the first chapter of Genesis where Elohim created His image and likeness both male and female, when it came to women, Tertullian, like most pre-orthodox and orthodox theologians for the next 18 centuries, ironically switched from the first chapter to the second of Genesis where only Adam, but not Eve, is made in the image and likeness of the all masculine Lord God Jehovah. David F. Noble in his *A World Without Women*, describes Tertullian's position of women in the church:

> Tertullian of Carthage also attacked Marcion for allowing women to become priests and even bishops within his church, and railed out against the women themselves as well. "These heretical women—how audacious they are! They have no modesty; they are bold enough to teach, to engage in argument, to enact exorcisms, to undertake cures, and, it may

be, even to baptize!" To contrast orthodox practice with such heretical habits, Tertullian prescribed what he regarded as "the precepts of ecclesiastical discipline concerning women," according to which "it is not permitted for a woman to speak in the church, nor is it permitted for her to teach, nor to baptize, nor to offer [the eucharist], nor to claim for herself a share in any masculine function—not to mention any priestly office."[4]

If God is Mother as well as Father, shouldn't His image and likeness be feminine as well as masculine? What can defy such logic except for the influence of either arrogance or patriarchic seduction? If the image and likeness is both male and female as declared in Genesis 1, why is half of humanity treated otherwise?

Dr. H. Paul Santmire, a historian and pastoral scholar and author, is concerned about the patriarchal interpretation of "Our Father" in the Lord's Prayer. He says that the "patriarchal shape" changes the meaning of the term *Abba* as used in Palestine in Jesus day, a term for a gentle, caring parent. He does not prefer the term *Father-Mother* as used by the nineteenth-century writer and church founder Mary Baker Eddy. He favors translating the first words of Jesus' prayer as "Our Parent."[5] Some feminine writers would disagree with avoiding a deity with both masculine and feminine aspects.

Dr. Virginia Ramey Mollenkott, a former English professor who has authored or co-authored 13 books, including ones on women and religion, would agree with Santmire that there is a problem with the patriarchal interpretation of "Our Father" in the Lord's Prayer, but instead of advocating "Our Parent," she calls for "Our Father and Mother in heaven." She bases this Father-Mother relationship upon the first two verses of Psalms 123:

> 1 Unto thee lift I up mine eyes, O thou that dwellest in the heavens.

> 2 Behold, as the eyes of servants look unto the hand of their masters, and as the eyes of a maiden unto the hand of her mistress; so our eyes wait upon the Lord our God...

Here is her logical thought:

> Yahweh is, then, not only our Father and Master
> who is in heaven, but also our Mother and Mistress
> who is in heaven. If anyone needs any scriptural
> authorization to address the Lord's prayer to both
> Father and Mother, Psalm 123:1-2, with its male-
> female parallelism concerning the divine, would
> seem to provide that sanction. The addition would
> not constitute a judgment on the teaching of Jesus,
> as if he should have said "Our Father and Mother"
> in the first place. Because Jesus was living in a
> patriarchal culture, calling for truly *stupendous*
> changes, he had to speak in terminology that the
> people could grasp. The more unfamiliar and radical
> the concept, the more familiar and unthreatening
> the language had better be! Jesus *modelled* the full
> equality of males and females; to have introduced
> directly a female image of God would at the time have
> been misunderstood as a reversion to paganism's
> multiplicity of divinities. Jesus did utilize word-
> pictures of God as female... But one good thing
> about word-pictures is that their significance does
> not dawn upon anybody who is not ready or able to
> receive them. Jesus' cultural surroundings made
> "Our Father and Mother in heaven" an impossibility;
> our cultural surroundings make it not only possible
> but necessary.[6]

In 1983, the National Council of the Churches of Christ also recognizes the gentle, non-patriarchic nature of *Abba*: "*Abba* is an accessible, caring, revered figure."[7] In the first of three lectionaries, the Council includes feminine terminology to accompany the masculine in order to avoid any patriarchic connotations for *Abba*. The Council does so by inserting the feminine italicized in brackets as optional in oral reading. The Lord's Prayer (Matthew 6:9-13) is not included in this volume, but a few verses beforehand, we read: "Beware of practicing your piety before others in order to be seen by them; for you will have no reward from [*God*] your Father [*and Mother*] who is in heaven" (Matthew 6:1).[8]

In 1995, the Oxford University Press copyrights and publishes a new version of the New Testament. The first two lines of the Lord's Prayer read:

> Our Father-Mother in heaven,
> Hallowed be your name.
>
> (Matthew 6:9)[9]

As a matter of fact, the term "Father-Mother" is used often. Bishop Krister Stendahl of Harvard University writes that this version "should be read as an important step in the search for a new inclusive idiom."[10]

So Santimire, Mollenkott, and the Oxford University Press agree that "Our Father" in the Lord's Prayer has taken on a patriarchal interpretation. The National Council of the Churches of Christ, from its lectionary indication a few verses before the Lord's Prayer, would appear to agree, too. The point is that when one prays "Our Father," one should *think* "Our Parent" or "Our Father and Mother" or "Our Father-Mother" or "Our Father-Mother God" or "Our Non-patriarchal Father" to get today the gentle, caring meaning meant by Jesus and Apostolic Christianity instead of the patriarchic interpretation of what we soon will see to be in this chapter, Aristotelian Christianity.

7. In Luke 15, we have three parables in a row, sometimes called the three parables of grace. The first deals with a shepherd who has lost one sheep of his hundred. The second has a woman who has lost one of her ten pieces of silver. And the third presents the father and his prodigal son. In all three there is "joy in heaven over one sinner that repenteth" than over all those who were never lost:

3 And he [Jesus] spake this parable unto them, saying,

4 What man of you, having an hundred sheep, if he lose one of them, doth not leave the ninety and nine in the wilderness, and go after that which is lost, until he find it?

5 And when he hath found it, he layeth it on his shoulders, rejoicing.

42

6 And when he cometh home, he calleth together his friends and neighbours, saying unto them, Rejoice with me; for I have found my sheep which was lost.

7 I say unto you, that likewise joy shall be in heaven over one sinner that repenteth, more than over ninety and nine just persons, which need no repentance.

8 Either what woman having ten pieces of silver, if she lose one piece, doth not light a candle, and sweep the house, and seek diligently till she find it?

9 And when she hath found it, she calleth her friends and her neighbours together, saying, Rejoice with me; for I have found the piece which I had lost.

10 Likewise, I say unto you, there is joy in the presence of the angels of God over one sinner that repenteth.

11 And he said, A certain man had two sons:

12 And the younger of them said to his father, Father, give me the portion of goods that falleth to me. And he divided unto them his living.

13 And not many days after the younger son gathered all together, and took his journey into a far country, and there wasted his substance with riotous living.

14 And when he had spent all, there arose a mighty famine in that land; and he began to be in want.

15 And he went and joined himself to a citizen of that country; and he sent him into his fields to feed swine.

16 And he would fain have filled his belly with the husks that the swine did eat: and no man gave unto him.

17 And when he came to himself, he said, How many hired servants of my father's have bread enough and to spare, and I perish with hunger!

18 I will arise and go to my father, and will say unto him, Father, I have sinned against heaven, and before thee,

19 And am no more worthy to be called thy son: make me as one of thy hired servants.

20 And he arose, and came to his father. But when he was yet a great way off, his father saw him, and had compassion, and ran, and fell on his neck, and kissed him.

21 And the son said unto him, Father, I have sinned against heaven, and in thy sight, and am no more worthy to be called thy son.

22 But the father said to his servants, Bring forth the best robe, and put it on him; and put a ring on his hand, and shoes on his feet:

23 And bring hither the fatted calf, and kill it; and let us eat, and be merry:

24 For this my son was dead, and is alive again; he was lost, and is found. ...

Commentators have no problem discussing the first and third parables. In the first, God is compared to a shepherd. In the third, He is compared to a father. The problem male theologians have is with the second where God is compared to a woman. Not just any woman, but a powerful one with money. Even though God is often compared to a woman in the Old Testament, male Christian theologians squirm with this feminine presentation of God in the new, even though it is their own Christ putting forth the idea. Is this squirming the result of either male arrogance or patriarchic seduction?

8. In the Gospel of John, first from chapter 1 and then 3, Jesus described the process of repenting as being born again as an innocent one straight from God.

12 But as many as received him [Jesus], to them gave he power to become the sons of God, even to them that believe on his name:

13 Which were born, not of blood, nor of the will of the flesh, nor of the will of man, but of God.

1 There was a man of the Pharisees, named Nicodemus, a ruler of the Jews:

2 The same came to Jesus by night, and said unto him, Rabbi, we know that thou art a teacher come from God: for no man can do these miracles that thou doest, except God be with him.

3 Jesus answered and said unto him, Verily, verily, I say unto thee, Except a man be born again, he cannot see the kingdom of God.

4 Nicodemus saith unto him, How can a man be born when he is old? can he enter the second time into his mother's womb, and be born?

5 Jesus answered, Verily, verily, I say unto thee, Except a man be born of water and of the Spirit, he cannot enter into the kingdom of God.

6 That which is born of the flesh is flesh; and that which is born of the Spirit is spirit.

7 Marvel not that I said unto thee, Ye must be born again.

8 The wind bloweth where it listeth, and thou hearest the sound thereof, but canst not tell whence it cometh, and whither it goeth: so is every one that is born of the Spirit.

Since the male cannot give birth, being born of the Spirit is being compared to being born from a female source. Outside of Jesus' referencing the Deity of the Old Testament as Spirit, the patriarchy of Jesus' day would not allow him otherwise to preach about God outright except to call the Deity *Abba*, the then current term for God, nowadays interpreted as the patriarchal Father. Can a male be a father without a mother to give birth to a child? Can a mother be a mother without both the male and the resulting child? In the birthing metaphor, is Jesus indirectly comparing Spirit, God, to Mother? Is to say otherwise a manifestation of patriarchic seduction?

In conclusion on this Jesus section, the Master Christian defied the traditions of his time by not only conversing with women in public but also teaching them religious lessons. He not only loved and respected women but also metaphorically implied that God is feminine as well as masculine.

Gnostic Christianity carried forward Jesus' equality of women, as seen in the *Gospel of Mary* (*Magdalene*), but pre-orthodox Christianity attacked Gnostic Christianity's notion that there are two creators, God who created good and an eon who created evil, thus eventually eradicating one of maybe two major Christian branches that treated the sexes as equals. Also, since Gnostic Christianity downplayed Simon Peter, the masculine-oriented, pre-orthodox Christianity needed to salvage Peter as their masculine leader. Consequently, Mary Magdalene was made a whore and Peter a saint. Only recently has the Catholic Church acknowledged that Jesus' casting seven devils out of Mary Magdalene does not mean she was a whore but probably was healed of various infirmities.

## Plato's Views of Women

Plato (428-348 B.C.E.) was a Greek philosopher and father of idealism. Little is known about his personal life. As a young man he was devoted to his Athenian friend Socrates and founded the first great philosophical school called the Academy, which, with perhaps a few interruptions, he administered and taught in until his death. Of his various writings, the *Republic* is the most famous.

In it, using the Socratic method of reasoning, he thinks through what he came to believe would be the perfect state, a utopia. His idealistic views—especially his proposal of equality of women and his plan of common ownership, including wives and children, for an educated, physically fit elite called the Guardians—have choked many men for over two millenniums.

Plato wrote in the same style of dialogue that his teacher Socrates used in teaching. Below, Plato either quoted or made up a dialogue between Socrates and another student, Glaucon (a Plato relative). Instead of using a concise lecture, Socrates used what has become known as the Socratic method: a drawn-out dialogue of questions and answers between teacher and student until the student had reasoned his way to the desired point. In the dialogue below, the paragraphs rotate between Socrates and Glaucon. However, since confusion can occur, I have labeled the paragraphs "S:" for Socrates and "G:" for Glaucon.

S: Which do we think right for watch-dogs: should the females guard the flock and hunt with the males and take a share in all they do, or should they be kept within doors as fit for no more than bearing and feeding their puppies, while all the hard work of looking after the flock is left to the males?

G: They are expected to take their full share, except that we treat them as not quite so strong.

S: Can you employ any creature for the same work as another, if you do not give them both the same upbringing and education?

G: No.

S: Then, if we are to set women to the same tasks as men, we must teach them the same things. They must have the same two branches of training for mind and body and also be taught the art of war, and they must receive the same treatment.

G: That seems to follow.

S: Possibly, if these proposals were carried out, they might be ridiculed as involving a good many breaches of custom.

G: They might indeed.

S: The most ridiculous—don't you think?—being the notion of women exercising naked along with the men in the wrestling-schools; some of them elderly women too, like the old men who still have a passion for exercise when they are wrinkled and not very agreeable to look at.

G: Yes, that would be thought laughable, according to our present notions.

S: Now we have started on this subject, we must not be frightened of the many witticisms that might be aimed at such a revolution, not only in the matter of bodily exercise but in the training of women's minds, and not least when it comes to their bearing arms and riding on horseback. Having begun upon these rules, we must not draw back from the harsher provisions. The wits may be asked to stop being witty and try to be serious; and we may remind them that it is not so long since the Greeks, like most foreign nations of the present day, thought it ridiculous and shameful for men to be seen naked. When gymnastic exercises were first introduced in Crete and later at Sparta, the humorists had their chance to make fun of them; but when experience had shown that nakedness is better uncovered than muffled up, the laughter died down and a practice which the reason approved ceased to look ridiculous to the eye. This shows how idle it is to think anything ludicrous but what is base. One who tries to raise a laugh at any spectacle save that of baseness and folly will also, in his serious moments, set before himself some other standard than goodness of what deserves to be held in honour.

G: Most assuredly.

S: The first thing to be settled, then, is whether these proposals are feasible; and it must be open to anyone, whether a humorist or serious-minded, to raise the question whether, in the case of mankind, the feminine nature is capable of taking part with the other sex in all occupations, or in none at all, or in some only; and in particular under which of these heads this business of military service falls. Well begun is half done, and would not this be the best way to begin?

G: Yes.

S: Shall we take the other side in this debate and argue against ourselves? We do not want the adversary's position to be taken by storm for lack of defenders.

G: I have no objection.

S: Let us state his case for him. "Socrates and Glaucon," he will say, "there is no need for others to dispute your position; you yourselves, at the very outset of founding your commonwealth, agreed that everyone should do the one work for which nature fits him." Yes, of course; I suppose we did. "And isn't there a very great difference in nature between man and woman?" Yes, surely. "Does not that natural difference imply a corresponding difference in the work to be given to each?" Yes. "But if so, surely you must be mistaken now and contradicting yourselves when you say that men and women, having such widely divergent natures, should do the same things?" What is your answer to that, my ingenious friend?

G: It is not easy to find one at the moment. I can only appeal to you to state the case on our own side, whatever it may be.

S: This, Glaucon, is one of many alarming objections which I foresaw some time ago. That is why I shrank from touching upon these laws concerning the possession of wives and the rearing of children.

G: It looks like anything but an easy problem.

S: True, I said; but whether a man tumbles into a swimming-pool or into mid-ocean, he has to swim all the same. So must we, and try if we can reach the shore, hoping for some Arion's [Greek poet who, when forced to jump into the sea, was saved and carried to shore by a dolphin] dolphin or other miraculous deliverance to bring us safe to land.

G: I suppose so.

S: Come then, let us see if we can find the way out. We did agree that different natures should have different occupations, and that the natures of man and woman are different; and yet we are now saying that these different natures are to have the same occupations. Is that the charge against us?

G: Exactly.

S: It is extraordinary, Glaucon, what an effect the practice of debating has upon people.

G: Why do you say that?

S: Because they often seem to fall unconsciously into mere disputes which they mistake for reasonable argument, through being unable to draw the distinctions proper to their subject; and so, instead of a philosophical exchange of ideas, they go off in chase of contradictions which are purely verbal.

G: I know that happens to many people; but does it apply to us at this moment?

S: Absolutely. At least I am afraid we are slipping unconsciously into a dispute about words. We have been strenuously insisting on the letter of our principle that different natures should not have the same occupations, as if we were scoring a point in a debate; but we have altogether neglected to consider what sort of sameness or difference we meant and in what respect these natures and occupations were to be defined as different or the same. Consequently, we might very well be asking one another whether there is not an opposition in nature between bald and long-haired men, and, when that was admitted, forbid one set to be shoemakers, if the other were following that trade.

G: That would be absurd.

S: Yes, but only because we never meant any and every sort of sameness or difference in nature, but the sort that was relevant to the occupations in question. We meant, for instance, that a man and a woman have the same nature if both have a talent for medicine; whereas two men have different natures if one is a born physician, the other a born carpenter.

G: Yes, of course.

S: If, then, we find that either the male sex or the female is specially qualified for any particular form of occupation, then that occupation, we shall say, ought to be assigned to one sex or the other. But if the only difference appears to be that the male begets and females brings forth, we shall conclude that no difference between man and woman has yet been produced that is relevant to our purpose. We shall continue to think it proper for our Guardians and their wives to share in the same pursuits.

G: And quite rightly.

S: The next thing will be to ask our opponent to name any profession or occupation in civic life for the purpose of which woman's nature is different from man's.

G: That is a fair question.

S: He might reply, as you did just now, that it is not easy to find a satisfactory answer on the spur of the moment, but that there would be no difficulty after a little reflection.

G: Perhaps.

S: Suppose, then, we invite him to follow us and see if we can convince him that there is no occupation concerned with the management of social affairs that is peculiar to women. We will confront him with a question: When you speak of man having a natural talent for something, do you mean that he finds it easy to learn, and after a little instruction can find out much more for himself; whereas a man who is not so gifted learns with difficulty and no amount of instruction and practice will make him even remember what he has been taught? Is the talented man one whose bodily powers are readily at the service of his mind, instead of being a hindrance? Are not these the marks by which you distinguish the presence of natural gift for any pursuit?

G: Yes, precisely.

S: Now do you know of any human occupation in which the male sex is not superior to the female in all these respects? Need I waste time over exceptions like weaving and watching over saucepans and batches of cakes, though women are supposed to be good at such things and get laughed at when a man does them better?

G: It is true, he replied, in almost everything one sex is easily beaten by the other. No doubt many women are better at many things than many men; but taking the sexes as a whole, it is as you say.

S: To conclude, then, there is no occupation concerned with the management of social affairs which belongs either to woman or to man, as such. Natural gifts are to be found here and there in both creatures alike; and every occupation is open to both, so far as their natures are concerned, though woman is for all purposes the weaker.

G: Certainly.

S: Is that a reason for making over all occupations to men only?

G: Of course not.

S: No, because one woman may have a natural gift for medicine or for music, another may not.

G: Surely.

S: Is it not also true that a woman may, or may not, be warlike or athletic?

G: I think so.

S: And again, one may love knowledge, another hate it; one may be high-spirited, another spiritless?

G: True again.

S: It follows that one woman will be fitted by nature to be a Guardian, another will not; because these were the qualities for which we selected our men Guardians. So for the purpose of keeping watch over the commonwealth, woman has the same nature as man, save in so far as she is weaker.

G: So it appears.

S: It follows that women of this type must be selected to share the life and duties of Guardians with men of the same type, since they are competent and of a like nature, and the same natures must be allowed the same pursuits.

G: Yes.

S: We came round, then, to our former position, that there is nothing contrary to nature in giving our Guardians' wives the same training for mind and body. The practice we proposed to establish was not impossible or visionary, since it was in accordance with nature. Rather, the contrary practice which now prevails turns out to be unnatural.

G: So it appears.

S: Well, we set out to inquire whether the plan we proposed was feasible and also the best. That it is feasible is now agreed; we must next settle whether it is the best.

G: Obviously.

S: Now, for the purpose of producing a woman fit to be a Guardian, we shall not have one education for men and another for women, precisely because the nature to be taken in hand is the same.

G: True.

S: What is your opinion on the question of one man being better than another? Do you think there is no such difference?

G: Certainly I do not.

S: And in this commonwealth of ours, which will prove the better men—the Guardians who have received the education we described, or the shoemakers who have been trained to make shoes?

G: It is absurd to ask such a question.

S: Very well. So these Guardians will be the best of all the citizens?

G: By far.

S: And these women the best of all the women?

G: Yes.

S: Can anything be better for a commonwealth than to produce in it men and women of the best possible type?

G: No.

S: And that result will be brought about by such a system of mental and bodily training as we have described?

G: Surely.

S: We may conclude that the institution we proposed was not only practicable, but also the best for the commonwealth.

G: Yes.

S: The wives of our Guardians, then, must strip for exercise, since they will be clothed with virtue, and they must take their share in war and in the other social duties of guardianship. They are to have no other occupation; and in these duties the lighter part must fall to the women, because of the weakness of their sex. The man who laughs at naked women, exercising their bodies for the best of reasons, is like one that "gathers fruit unripe," for he does not know what it is that he is laughing at or what he is doing. There will never be a finer saying than the one which declares that whatever does good should be held in honour, and the only shame is in doing harm.

G: That is perfectly true.[11]

Let's consider several questions concerning Plato's views of women:

1. Plato's *Republic* presented a communistic view of society for the Guardians in which everything is held in common—property, wives, and children. His views went much further than those found in the communism that was in Russia and that is in China. According to Plato, the ideal situation for a woman would include the following: (1) Own all the community's property in common with everyone else. (2) At various times be the wife to various men in the community—as long as any union of the sexes is regulated by the Rulers for the best breeding results, one wife at a time per a good male breeder, either none or a poor breeding wife for a poor breeding husband, and each good breeding woman (one who had bore a child that year) up for an annual marriage reconsideration. And (3) have her children taken from her at birth to be reared by the perfect state (with no mother nursing her own child and every "defective" child taken out of the community of Guardians).[12]

   Would a woman of today want to live under Plato's suggested conditions? How would most women today feel if their baby was taken away from them at birth and they were forced to nurse someone else's baby? Is marriage only about breeding?[13] What about the love and feelings between a man and woman? Should the state be making such decisions regarding the family? Jesus advocated a man and woman's marrying for life. Which position—Jesus' or Plato's—would be better for the mental health of the child, the security of the woman, the stability of the man?

2. In Plato's communism, only the men and women of the elite Guardians were politically equal. Those who were called

craftsmen or had some physical defect were not equal to the elite nor were the sexes equal. To paraphrase a comment in the novel *Animal Farm*, all people are equal, but some people are more equal than others. As stated on the Molloy College website, "In a sense, Plato's communal/communistic approach is similar to that of religious orders during the Middle Ages. It was believed that if a monk owned nothing of his own, he would be able to devote himself totally to God. Similarly, Plato believes that Guardians will be able to commit themselves totally and completely to the good of the city [Athens], because they have no material distractions."[14] A major difference between the pagan's communism and the Christian's communism is that with the Christian one the monks were equal but the women were kept out of the religious community and treated more like the women in the craftman's class in Plato's scheme of things. There was no political, religious, or educational equality of the sexes in the Christian's communism. Plato envisioned the equality of women in an elitist, communistic society. Can the equality of women be obtained under such a twisted form of government?

3. It was customary in Socrates' day for Greek men to exercise in the nude and practice the art of war in the nude. Likewise, reasoned Socrates, if women are equal, they should be treated equally: in the Guardian community, they should strip and join the men in these two activities. Furthermore, he said that if any man should laugh at such a woman, he would be revealing his own ignorance.

   Would women like this level of equality? Some women opposed the Equal Rights Amendment to the U.S. Constitution some years ago for fear that equality would dictate equal military service of the sexes. Where should the line be drawn in determining complete equality of the sexes? Does equality mean that women have to be more masculine and do more masculine things, or does equality mean that feminine qualities are valued as much as masculine ones so that all people have access to both sets of qualities?

   In conclusion for the Plato section, this ancient Greek philosopher advocated an equality of the sexes for an elite few in which everyone in this segment of society owned everything in common except for the current spouse, who could be exchanged for the good of the state about every twelve months to ensure good breeding. The Rulers were to determine who was to mate with whom. Of course, equality of the sexes among common people was not even considered. But do Plato's ideas offer true equality of males and females even among the elite few?

The communistic elite adopted in Christianity were the male clergy and monks. Patriarchy excluded women from the chosen. With Jesus' teaching of equality of the sexes already rejected, it wasn't difficult for patriarchic Christianity to adapt Plato's concept of equality so that it benefited only men. Plato's proposed equality of the sexes was to be for the good of the state. Patriarchic Christianity's inequality was believed to be for the good of the patriarchic Church.

About six to eight hundred years after St. Augustine Christianized Plato in the fourth century, Plato's ideas were newly revived in Christianity. Plato's acceptance of homosexuality and his emphasis on sex among those in the elite appear to have been translated to widespread acceptance of homosexuality among the Christian elite, the clergy and monks, for about two hundred years.[15] (This point is not made to ostracize gay men. The point is that the religious leaders had taken a vow of chastity, of celibacy, which means no sex with men as well as women. It applied to both heterosexual and homosexual clergy.)

Then about four hundred years later in the seventeenth century, Plato's emphasis on proper breeding appeared to evolve in efforts to "breed" without the aid of women. Suffice it to say, however, the adopted ideas from a pagan philosopher had changed Christianity.

## Aristotle's Views of Women

Aristotle (384-322 B.C.E.) is father of deductive logic, characterized by the syllogism (major premise plus minor premise yields conclusion). He was mostly a man of science and, consequently, of inductive reasoning, also. At age seventeen, he went to Athens to study under Plato. When Plato died twenty years later, Aristotle was passed over as the person to replace Plato as head of the

Academy: Aristotle's mind was considered too divergent from Plato's. Disappointed, he traveled to Asia Minor to retreat in the court of his philosophical friend, Hermeas, whose niece Aristotle married. When Aristotle was forty-two, Philip of Macedon summoned him to tutor his fifteen-year-old son, who would later become known as Alexander the Great. However, when Philip was assassinated, Aristotle went back to Athens and began the Peripatetic school as a rivalry to the Platonic Academy. It was here at his new school that he probably wrote his philosophy and science books that still survive. As the son of a physician, he had learned how to dissect both human and animal corpses. His drawings are very detailed. In his writings, he was not concerned with artistic form or literary style. Instead, he tried to adhere "to essential naked truth." His writings revived an interest in science, although scientific research didn't really start to evolve until about 1700 years later during the Renaissance. Somehow, consequently, the man of logic and careful observations missed content, as well as artistic form, when it came to women—and, some say, also to sheep, goats, swine, sparrows, etc. The following passages from Aristotle's writings illustrate his diabolical views of women. They are important because St. Thomas Aquinas Christianized Aristotle's ideas in the thirteenth century, and this pagan Greek philosopher's ideas of women still dominate in much of Western Christianity.[16]

1.  Let's begin Aristotle's views of women:

> The nature of man is the most rounded off and complete . . . Hence woman is more compassionate than man, more easily moved to tears, at the same time is more jealous, more querulous [apt to complain], more apt to scold and to strike. She is, furthermore, more prone to despondency and less hopeful than the man, more void of shame or self-respect, more false of speech, more deceptive, and of more retentive memory. She is also more wakeful, more shrinking, more difficult to rouse to action, and requires a smaller quantity of nutriment.[17]

> Now if the above is a description of Aristotle's wife, I feel sorry for the man. And since the patriarchic culture of Aristotle's day offered women few rights, might women

naturally have been "more jealous," "less hopeful," "more shrinking"? Furthermore, since patriarchy also still strangles men from shedding tears, might women naturally be "more easily moved to tears"? Whatever the case, it is hard to believe that the man known for his logic would have made such a sweeping generalization that all women are "more false of speech, more deceptive," in addition to other questionable accusations. I have known men who are "more false of speech, more deceptive." It is not a gender issue. We probably might agree that "woman is more compassionate than man" (at least he conceded something in her favor) and "requires a smaller quantity of nutriment." Any man writing the above passage today might find women television hosts advocating that his head be pitched like a softball across home plate.

2.  Aristotle's ignorance of biology is apparent:

> The female is, as it were, a mutilated male, and the catamenia [menstrual discharges] are semen, only not pure; for there is only one thing they [catamenia] have not in them, the principle of soul [which is carried by the male semen only. Note: Eggs in humans were not discovered until 1827.][18]

Two syllogisms are apparent here. The first deals with the ancient belief that menstrual discharges are red semen:

**Major Premise:** Any human who does not secret white semen, the source of life and soul, is an inferior being.
**Minor Premise:** Women secrete red semen.
**Conclusion:** Therefore, women are inferior to men.

The second syllogism also deals with an ancient belief: women are mutilated or undeveloped men:

**Major Premise:** Any human without male reproductive organs is an incomplete, undeveloped human and is thus inferior to a person with such organs.

**Minor Premise:** Women do not have male reproductive organs.

**Conclusion:** Therefore, women are inferior to men.

Both of these Major Premises and the first Minor Premise are false beliefs, yet both therefore false Conclusions still permeate Western theology and thus much of Western thought.

St. Thomas Aquinas is known for many great ideas concerning Deity, especially when he stayed focused on the Bible. But when it came to women, he stayed focused on Aristotle. He quoted this passage above as one the Aristotelians of his time used to justify the inequality of men and women. Aquinas agreed with this notion but disagreed with their extreme idea that God should not have made woman.[19] Furthermore, based upon Aristotle, Aquinas reasoned that women—defective, inferior, and impure creatures because of their menstrual cycles, thus being unfinished men—are subordinate to men and consequently not fit to be ordained as Christian priests.[20] Later in his writings, with the subordination of women already well fixed in thought from Aristotle, Aquinas also used a combination of mistranslation and second-century forgery of St. Paul to make a similar not-fit-for-priesthood claim.

3. Aristotle's ignorance of biology continues:

For more females are produced by the young and by those verging on old age than by those in the prime of life; in the former the vital heat is not yet perfect, in the latter it is failing. And those of a moister and more feminine state of body are more wont to beget females. . .[21]

Humanity back then had not learned that male semen determines the sex of a child, not as the ancients believed that the sex depended upon the mother's "vital heat" or upon how much moisture she had.

St. Thomas Aquinas quoted this passage as another one the Aristotelians used to show that women are "defective and misbegotten." It is not certain just how much Aquinas agreed with this Aristotelianism because just before this reference, Aquinas said that as soon as God made woman, the man and his wife were one flesh (Genesis 2:24). A man wouldn't have wanted to become one flesh with something *too* defective.[22] Compare Aquinas' quote of "one flesh" with Jesus' earlier in this chapter. Aquinas' does not carry the equality that Jesus was expressing. Jesus did not mix this biblical quote with suggestions that women were "defective and misbegotten."

4. Now, dear reader, prepare your loins for laughter:

Males have more teeth than females in the case of men, sheep, goats, and swine; in the case of other animals observations have not yet been made; but the more teeth they have the more long-lived are they, as a rule, while those are short-lived in proportion that have teeth fewer in number and thinly set.[23]

The last teeth to come in man are molars called "wisdom-teeth," which come at the age of twenty years, in the case of both sexes. Cases have been known in women upwards of eighty years old where at the very close of life the wisdom-teeth have come up, causing great pain in their coming; and cases have been known of the like phenomenon in men too. This happens, when it does happen, in the case of people where the wisdom-teeth have not come up in early years.[24]

Aristotle obviously made some false claims of the number of teeth males and females have. The following information should help you put what he said in proper perspective. (1) Men and women have the same number of teeth, 32, although some women lose a tooth or two with each child they bear. A dentist told me it is very rare that an eighty-year-old person will have the belated cutting in of wisdom teeth. Such an event might have occurred more often, though still rarely, in Aristotle's time; food of ancient Greece might have been more gritty than our food, thus slowly grinding down the teeth, a process that will make the teeth smaller, have them move forward, and thus allow room for wisdom teeth finally to come in. However, this process, though rare, when it does happen, occurs equally between men and women.[25] (2) Both male and female sheep have 24 teeth. (3) Both male and female goats have 32 teeth. However, it may take a goat up to five years to cut all of its teeth. (4) Both male and female swine have 44 teeth. (5) A veterinarian did some research for me. He found that in mammals, both the male and female of each species have the same number of teeth. There can be, however, some variation in horses where both males and females may have 40 or 42 teeth. Also, the mare's canines sometimes are so small that they don't cut through the gums, thus giving the appearance that she has only 36 or 38 teeth. He wonders whether, since research was so unscientific in ancient Greece, someone looked into the mouth of a few horses and then made a generalization about all mammals, including humans.[26]

Is Aristotle's discussion of teeth a case of assumptions being recorded as facts (he said it was based on observations), of some unbelievable chance that every sample of humans, sheep, goats, and swine was a rare variation from the norm, or of the falsifying of data to support some preconceived idea? He went into a long explanation of a rare condition of eighty-year-old women painfully cutting wisdom teeth and then as in an aside mentioned that the phenomenon had also been observed in men. Since this rare condition occurs equally with men and women, why do you think that Aristotle didn't simply refer to this abnormality in *people* instead of focusing on women with an aside about men?

Aristotle was implying that the more teeth one has, the more superior one is. Let's examine his faulty syllogism:

> **Major Premise:** The number of teeth in a species determines superiority and inferiority.
> **Minor Premise:** In humans, sheep, goats, and swine, males have more teeth than females.
> **Conclusion:** Therefore, males are superior to females.

Now if you are not laughing so hard that your eyes are closed and watering, let's think through this syllogism by the man known for his logic. First, the implication that produced the Major Premise is not based upon either science or logic. Can it be an example of pure arrogance? Let's face it; if the number of teeth is so important in determining worth, then we humans are equal with goats, both having 32 teeth. And God save us, for we must be inferior to pigs, which have 44 teeth! Second, the Minor Premise is false, an outright lie. How about adding arrogance here, too? And third, if arrogance begets a lie and more arrogance, what do these beget in a Conclusion that says males are superior to females or, in the negative, females are inferior to males? This is so laughable except that Aristotle was the one man whose ideas were Christianized in the thirteenth century and whose conclusions about women still rule in most of Western Christianity today! Thus we see the results when a Christian theologian substituted the opinions of a pagan philosopher for those of the Christian Master!

Dr. Garry Wills, professor of history, himself a Catholic, writes in his book *Papal Sin*, in the chapter titled "Excluded Women,"

> ... there is nothing in the gospels to indicate that Jesus himself could have held any of the vile attitudes about female inferiority and impurity that we have seen the church's teachers displaying through the centuries and imposing in his name. Those views were foisted on him—by bishops, and theologians, and saints who thought they knew better than the gospel. They were preaching Aristotle, not Christ.[27]

5. Now Aristotle justifies the political inequality of women:

> Democracy is the least bad . . . form of constitution. . . . One may find resemblances to the constitutions and, as it were, patterns of them even in households. For the association of a father with his sons bears the form of monarchy, since the father cares for his children; and this is why Homer calls Zeus "father". . . . The association of man and wife seems to be aristocratic; for the man rules in accordance with his worth, and in those matters in which a man should rule, but the matters that befit a woman he hands over to her. If the man rules in everything the relation passes over into oligarchy [government ruled by few]; for in doing so he is not acting in accordance with their respective worth, and not ruling in virtue of his superiority. Sometimes, however, women rule, because they are heiresses; so their rule is not in

virtue or excellence but due to wealth and power, as in oligarchies.[28]

A husband and father, we saw, rules over wife and children, both free, but the rule differs, the rule over his children being a royal, over his wife a constitutional rule. For although there may be exceptions to the order of nature, the male is by nature fitter for command than the female, just as the elder and full-grown is superior to the younger and more immature. But in most constitutional states the citizens rule and are ruled by turns, for the idea of a constitutional state implies that the natures of the citizens are equal, and do not differ at all. Nevertheless, when one rules and the other is *ruled we endeavour to create a difference of outward forms and names and titles of respect.* [Emphasis added.] ... The relation of the male to the female is of this kind, but there the inequality is permanent.[29]

According to Aristotle, the best form of state government is democracy, but in the family, the man rules over the wife as in an aristocracy and over their children as in a monarchy. The man rules his wife because he is worth more and has more virtue. Aristotle believed that "the male is by nature fitter for command than the female" and that the male-female "inequality is permanent."

That word *command* really indicates a male-dominated society. The connotation implies complete and immediate obedience as in either a military or police unit rather than a family unit as we know it today. Is there some arrogance in declaring that men are *worth* more than women and have more *virtue* than women? Such certainly does not sound like the teaching of Christ.

The Minor Premise in the following syllogism should be obviously false to anyone who has dealt with enough men and women and who understands human nature. Remember, false Premise yields false Conclusion.

**Major Premise:** Any human who is less virtuous than another is also inferior to the other.
**Minor Premise:** All men are more virtuous than all women.

**Conclusion:** Therefore, all men are superior to all women.

6. Aristotle holds his ground on the inferiority of women and attacks Plato's:

A . . . question may be raised about women and children, whether they too have virtues: ought a woman to be temperate and brave and just, and is a child to be called temperate, and intemperate, or not? So in general we may ask about the natural ruler, and the natural subject, whether they have the same or different virtues. . . . It is evident . . . that both of them must have a share of virtue, but varying as natural subjects also vary among themselves. Here the very constitution of the soul has shown us the way; in it one part naturally rules, and the other is subject, and the virtue of the ruler we maintain to be different from that of the subject;—the one being the virtue of the rational, and the other of the irrational part. Now, it is obvious that the same principle applies generally, and therefore almost all things rule and are ruled according to nature. But the kind of rule differs;—the freeman rules over the slave after another manner from that in which the male rules over the female, or the man over the child; although the parts of the soul are present in all of them, they are present in different degrees. For the slave has no deliberative faculty at all; the woman has, but it is without authority, and the child has, but it is immature. . . . [T]he temperance of a man and of a woman, or the courage and justice of a man and of a woman, are not, as Socrates maintained, the same; the courage of man is shown in commanding, of a woman in obeying. . . . All classes must be deemed to have their special attributes; as the poet [Sophocles] says of women,

*Silence is a woman's glory,*

but this is not equally the glory of man.[30]

The citizens might conceivably have wives and children and property in common, as Socrates proposes in the *Republic* of Plato. Which is better, our present condition, or the proposed new order of society?[31]

There are many difficulties in the community of women. And the principle on which Socrates rests the necessity of such an institution evidently is not established by his arguments.[32]

Again, if Socrates makes the women common, and retains private property, the men will see to the fields, but who will see to the house? And who will do so if the agricultural class have both their property and their wives in common? Once more: it is absurd to argue, from the analogy of the animals, that men and women should follow the same pursuits, for animals have not to manage a household.[33]

In the *Republic*, Socrates has definitely settled in all a few questions only; such as the community of women and children, the community of property, and constitution of the state. . . . He certainly thinks that the women ought to share in the education of the guardians, and to fight by their side. The remainder of the work is filled up with digressions foreign to the main subject, and with discussions about the education of the guardians.[34]

Aristotle wrote that a woman has "deliberate faculty" but lacks the authority to use it. Says who? Men? Is patriarchy the source for issuing or not issuing authority? Is there some male arrogance in here some place?

Aristotle disagreed with Plato or Socrates that the sexes are equal. He claimed that the temperance or courage of a man is in commanding and of a woman is in obeying. My guess is that some women readers just now sent their blood pressure soaring to complement their flushing, angry faces. In my own case, although I have had several good bosses over the years, the best one was a woman. She did not need to *command* like a man to be an effective *leader*, to draw all employees into a loyalty to her and the team's mission. She gently discussed things with either an individual or a group and naturally evoked a desire to accomplish a goal or mission. To me, *that* is more *worth*; *that* is more *virtue*. Men willingly *obeyed* both the team's direction and her suggestions with unparalleled allegiance and enthusiasm.

From my experience, I think that Aristotle's ideas about temperament are based upon a patriarchic educational system interwoven with several threads of arrogance. But I am apparently in a minority because Aristotle's views of temperament that a woman is meant to obey are interwoven throughout Western theology and culture, even in some marriage vows.

Aristotle furthermore implied that the sexes have to be unequal so that women will manage the household, or, he asked, who else will do it? If the husband is the breadwinner and the wife chooses to be a stay-home mother and manage the family, who says that the man and woman have to be unequal? Who says that household work is not work or is not an integral part of a partnership? Patriarchy? Men had better watch out now that our economy sometimes makes the woman the breadwinner and the husband the housekeeper. If both share the breadwinnership, should they, as equal partners, share the family chores? Those men who have already put this book aside, if they had not, probably now would be shuffling in their seats with an itchy, patriarchic bite on their butts.

Lastly on these passages, a Greek poet penned that "Silence is a woman's glory." Note that the poet was a man, of course.

7. Aristotle lays foundation for combining philosophy with theology:

> [For education,] there must . . . be three theoretical philosophies, mathematics, physics, and what we call theology, since it is obvious that if the divine is present anywhere, it is present in things of this sort.[35]

Thomas Aquinas used this passage from Aristotle to justify combining the teachings of philosophy, specifically of Aristotle's, with those of revelation to form the theology of Western Christianity and thus the philosophy of existence for the Western world.[36]

* * *

In short, Jesus defied the patriarchy of his day by not only speaking to women in public but by also teaching them the Scriptures and the Messianic message. Furthermore, many prominent women accompanied him and his male disciples on his journeys. And he taught that Elohim made His image and likeness both male and female. Patriarchic Christianity, however, rejected Jesus' position on women, as well as Plato's sense of equality. It did accept Plato's communistic views, but only for men in religious orders and teaching positions. These rejections of women's equality paved the way for the acceptance of Aristotle's syllogistically illogical, arrogant, false, diabolical ideas of women when Thomas Aquinas Christianized the writings of this ancient, pagan philosopher. Unfortunately, these diabolical views of women still reign in most of Western theology and culture.

Have you ever asked people why they believe a certain idea and they answered with a vague, uninvestigated comment like "because people have always believed that," or "because people have believed that for centuries"? What about some beliefs about women, the foundations for which have no scientific or logical bases? If people no longer accept the premises that led to these beliefs, what can be done to eradicate the beliefs themselves?

Since truth to Aristotle is that which can be deduced logically from what the senses report, he probably did not give much credence to what is called "women's intuition," although he certainly accepted his own preconceived ideas as truth. Do you believe in women's intuition? Can truth be learned through something other than logic and the senses?

I remember years ago, while standing in front of the microwave oven in my bathrobe and slippers, without hearing or seeing what had just happened outside, I jerked around to see my wife lying on the driveway from an apparent icy condition that had developed overnight. Still in my bathrobe and slippers, I rushed out to her in the cold. But where did the thought suddenly come from to turn and look outside? Intuition? If not, from where?

## Conclusion

In conclusion for this chapter, the women in some parts of the world have far fewer rights than Western women. What can be done, if anything, to help these foreign women? Some Islamic women see "the negative winds from the West"—a high divorce rate, alcoholism, drug addition, herpes, and AIDS—as threatening their security both in the home and in society. They reject the West's freedom of women as unstabilizing. How should we help liberate these women? Should we even try?

Does Jesus' admonishment apply here?

> 3 And why beholdest thou the mote that is in thy brother's eye, but considerest not the beam that is in thine own eye?

> 5 Thou hypocrite, first cast out the beam out of thine own eye; and then shalt thou see clearly to cast out the mote out of thy brother's eye. (Matthew 7)

Should not Christians and Jews look to see what they can do about these "negative winds from the West" that concern many Islamic people?

In this chapter, I have been discussing how patriarchy and the philosophies of Plato and Aristotle have influenced Christian theology and culture. But it is known that patriarchy and these two Greek philosophers have also influenced both Jewish and Islamic philosophy, theology, and culture. Are there any Jewish and Islamic scholars willing to help examine and excrete these influences from their own theologies and cultures?

As for Christians, it boils down to this: one's view of women in part depends upon whether one focuses on the reigning, patriarchic, pagan-Greek philosophically oriented view of women in Christianity or on Christ's sequestered views of women.

# Endnotes
## Chapter 3

1  J. R. Dummelow, *A Commentary on the Holy Bible*, Macmillan Publishing Co., New York, 1936, p.782.
2  *The Interpreter's Bible*, vol. VII of XII, New York: Abingdon-Cokesbury Press, 1952, p. 796, note.
3  *The Ante-Nicene Fathers*, tran. S. Thelwall, vol. III, p.682, online at http://www.earlychristianwritings.com/text/tertullian22.html.
4  David F. Noble, *A World Without Women*, New York: Alfred A. Knopf, 1992, p. 47.
5  H. Paul Santmire, "Retranslating 'Our Father': the Urgency and the Possibility," *Dialog*, vol. 16:2 (Spring 1977), pp. 101-106.

   Mark L. Strauss, a seminary New Testament professor, although not specifically addressing the first words of the Lord's Prayer, agrees that both the Hebrew and Greek words for *father* can be translated *parent*. See his *Distorting Scripture? The Challenge of Bible Translation & Gender Accuracy*, Downers Grove, IL: InterVarsity Press, 1998, pp. 42, 151,152.
6  Virginia Ramey Mollenkott, *The Divine Feminine: The Biblical Imagery of God as Female*, New York: Crossroad, 1983, p. 61.

   Dr. Karen Jo Torjesen, considered a leading authority on women in ancient Christianity, although not specifically addressing the first words of the Lord's Prayer, referred to God as mother, the forgiving mother. She also quoted a fourteenth century woman theologian, Dame Julian of Norwich in *Revelations of Divine Love*, "And then I saw that God rejoices that he is our Father; and God rejoices that he is our Mother; and God rejoices that he is our true Spouse, and that our soul is his beloved wife. And Christ rejoices that he is our Brother; and Jesus rejoices that he is our Savior. These are the five high joys." See Dr. Torjesen's book, *When Women Were Priests: Women's Leadership in the Early Church & the Scandal of Their Subordination in the Rise of Christianity*, New York: HarperOne, 1993, pp. 264, 265.
7  National Council of the Churches of Christ, *An Inclusive Language Lectionary: Readings of Year A*, Philadelphia: The Westminster Press, 1983, 3rd page of Appendix.
8  *Ibid.*, no page number given.

9 *The New Testament and Psalms: An Inclusive Version*, New York, New York: Oxford University Press, 1995, p. 9.

10 *Ibid.*, back side of jacket.

11 Excerpts from Plato's *Republic*, tran. by Francis Cornford [1874-1943], London: Oxford University Press, 1941, bk. v, pp. 451-457.

12 The Spartans killed "defective children," as did the Nazis, who also killed off anyone with mental problems and disabled adults in order to make room for wounded soldiers.

13 Plato's suggested methods did become employed by the Nazis to create a pure Aryan race.

14 http://www.molloy.edu/Sophia/plato/ republic/rep3b_comm. htm, p. 3 (3/28/2010).

15 Noble, pp. 134-135, 154-155, 172.

16 It is interesting to note that the great, gothic Chartres Cathedral in Chartres, France, was completed in 1260, when Thomas Aquinas was 35 years old. It is famous for its magnificent structure, beautiful windows, and its statues depicting figures from the Old and New Testaments, French kings and queens, and ancient Greek philosophers, including Aristotle.

17 Aristotle, *History of Animals*, bk. IX, chap. 1, trans. by D'Arcy Wentworth Thompson [1860-1948], in *The Works of Aristotle*, London: Oxford University Press, 1928.

18 Aristotle, *On the Generation of Animals*, bk. II, chap. 3, trans. by Arthur Platt [1860-1925], in *The Works of Aristotle*, London: Oxford University Press, 1928.

19 Thomas Aquinas, *Summa Theologica*, part. I, ques. 92, art.1, trans. by Fathers of the English Dominican Province, London: Burns, Oates & Washbourne, 1915-1922.

20 *Ibid.*, III Supplement, ques., 39, art. 1.

21 Aristotle, *On the Generation of Animals*, bk. IV, chap. 2.

22 Thomas Aquinas, *Summa Theologica*, part. I, ques. 92, art.1.

23 Aristotle, *History of Animals*, bk. II, chap.3.

24 *Ibid.*, chap. 4.

25 Telephonic interview with Dr. Pamela Weitzel about 2001.

26 Telephonic interview with Dr. Robert Furness about 2001.

   Since Dr. Furness mentioned horses, as well as the other animals in the Aristotelian quote at hand, he must have been aware that Aristotle did discuss horses' canines just before the quote I chose.

27 Garry Wills, *Papal Sin: Structures of Deceit*, New York: Doubleday, 2000, p. 114.

28 Aristotle, *Nicomachean Ethics*, bk. VIII, chap. 10, trans. by W.D. Ross [1877-1971], in *The Works of Aristotle*, London: Oxford University Press, 1928.

29 Aristotle, *Politics*, bk. I, chap. 12, trans. by Benjamin Jowett [1817-1893], in *The Works of Aristotle*, London: Oxford University Press, 1928.

30 *Ibid.*, bk. I, chap. 13.

31 *Ibid.*, bk. II, chap. 1.

32 *Ibid.*, bk. II, chap. 2.

33 *Ibid.*, bk. II, chap. 5.

34 *Ibid.*, bk. II, chap. 6.

35 Aristotle, *Metaphysics*, bk. VI, chap. 1, trans. by W.D. Ross [1877-1971], in *The Works of Aristotle*, London: Oxford University Press, 1928.

36 Thomas Aquinas, *Summa Theologica*, part. I, ques. 1, art.1.

# Chapter 4

## St. Paul's Teachings about Women

The Apostolic Church began with a continuation of Christ Jesus' exoneration of women. Men and women prayed together, as when they prayed "with one accord" to be led of God in choosing a replacement for Judas, the traitor (Acts 1:14+). "Multitudes both of men and women" were accepted as believers after the Day of Pentecost (Acts 5:14). When Philip preached in Samaria, he baptized "both men and women" (Acts 8:12). Christian women were considered such a vital part of what was called the Way—much different from the women in Judaism—that Saul, yet to be converted, persecuted both men and women of the Way (Acts 9:1-2; 22:4, 5).

After his conversion, Saul humbly took the name Paul, meaning "the little one." But this "little one" became a giant while following his Master in lifting women to new heights. The false and poor translations of some passages in his epistles, as seen through the eyes of patriarchic Christianity that had adopted Aristotle's diabolical ideas about women, and epistles written after Paul's death but ascribed to him, reversed some of Paul's positions on women and made them distorted in part, mixed at best. Thus some passages pertaining to women were twisted to sound more in accord with Aristotle's pagan views instead of Christ's uplifting ones. Many of these old mistranslations of Paul's writings, and forgeries written decades later in his name, considered either venerable or sacred, have thus been carried forward into many newer translations. In short, the Master's champion was, and has continued to be, translated and post-Paulinily pseudonymously manipulated into a patriarchal bigot.

To start, let's examine the place of women in the churches during Paul's lifetime. Dr. Margaret Y. MacDonald, Professor of New Testament at St. Francis Xavier University in Nova Scotia, Canada, points out that churches gathered in houses (e.g. Rom. 16:5; I Cor. 16:19; Phlm 2) and that

> scholars now recognize that because so important activity took place in a sphere traditionally associated with women, possibilities for women's involvement in leadership roles must have been greatly increased. Evidence from the Pauline corpus and from Acts which speaks of women as leaders of house-churches has been judged to be especially significant (Phlm 2; I Cor. 16.19; Rom. 16.5; Col. 4.15; Acts 16.14-15, 40).[1]

The purpose of this chapter is to examine what Paul wrote about men and women. To do this, we will have to remove the Aristotelian translating filter to find the Pauline thought in the epistles he did pen or dictate and also to separate the epistles that Paul actually wrote from those pseudonymously written at the end of the first century and during the second when the church was moving out of homes into the public and was more and more being influenced by ancient Greek pagan views of women.

One time my wife wanted to order some jewelry from Peru to match what our daughter had brought her from there. So she wrote out her letter in English and submitted it to an online translation program to put it in Spanish. When she showed the "Spanish" letter to someone who knew Spanish—oh, my—many changes were needed in the translation if she wanted the message to generate the desired jewelry. When Paul's epistles were translated into "English" centuries ago, it were as though they were put through some kind of pre-conceived Aristotelian translating program and—oh, my—there was no one from either Christ's or Paul's thinking available to clear up the message about women.

To get a clear picture of Paul's thought, let's start with a passage that did *not* get mistranslated: "There is neither Jew nor Greek, there is neither bond nor free, there is neither male nor female: for ye are all one in Christ Jesus" (Galatians 3:28). The message is straight forward: among Christians, there is equality among nationalities; there is equality among social classes; there is equality between the genders. Males and females were equal in the sight of Christ.

What a reversal of both Jewish and Greek religious beliefs and customs, which were definitely highly patriarchal! In both of these cultures, women had few if any rights. They were to remain obediently silent. In the synagogues women were to be located so that the men could not see them. Neither culture allowed women to gather in large groups to carry on womanly discussions. Now Paul comes along and says not so in Christianity. Men and women are equal, both made in the image and likeness of that God described in the first chapter of Genesis. It was difficult for the Aristotelian-minded translators to screw up this passage. So it got by unscathed and revealed the true Pauline position on women.

## Ephesians 5:20-25, 31, 33

Dr. Bart D. Ehrman, professor of Religious Studies at the University of North Carolina, Chapel Hill, and author of numerous books on the Bible, writes that today the majority of biblical scholars agree that the Book of Ephesians was *not* written by Paul. He gives four reasons why: (1) "The writing style is not Paul's. Paul usually writes in short, pointed sentences; the sentences in Ephesians are long and complex." As an example, Ehrman cites 1:3-14, twelve verses that make up one sentence. Furthermore, Ephesians "has an inordinate number of words that don't otherwise occur in Paul's writings". .... (2) Some points in Ephesians do not jive with what Paul writes in his undisputed letters. For example, in Ephesians Paul is made to say that before his conversion, he was consumed by the "passions of our flesh, doing the will of the flesh and senses." But in Philippians (3:4) he records that he had been "blameless" in the "righteousness of the law." Furthermore, Paul writes of salvation by faith and grace, but in Ephesians "the author does not speak about salvation apart from the 'works of the law.'" (3) Ephesians speaks of believers having already been "saved." But in Paul's writings salvation will come in the future. And (4) Paul writes of the resurrection being at the Second Coming of Christ; Ephesians, of it being now (2:5-6). If Paul wrote Ephesians, he had changed his writing style, facts about his pre-conversion activities, and part of his theology on salvation and the resurrection.[2]

Just as important, if not more so, are points Dr. MacDonald and her colleagues point out about the difference between Paul's ideas about the bride of Christ and instructions in marriage and those expressed in Ephesians. She joined Dr. Carolyn Osiek, professor of New Testament at Brite Divinity School, Fort Worth, Texas, and Dr. Janet H. Tulloch in a different book, *A Woman's Place: House Churches in Earliest Christianity*:

Links between communal identity and marriage are created in two main ways in the undisputed letters of Paul: through the symbolic depiction of the community as the bride of Christ (2 Cor. 11:2-3) and through instructions to marry with an attitude and attention to purity that separates the community from the immoral Gentile world (1 Thess. 4:4-5; 1 Cor. 7; compare 2 Cor. 6:14—7:1). In Ephesians, these two tendencies are brought together. The holiness, purity, and submission of the church as the bride who is loved by Christ (Eph. 5:23b, 25b-27, 29b) serves to justify and explain why wives should submit to the authority of their husbands and why husbands should love and cherish their wives (Eph. 5:22-23a, 24-25a, 28-29a, 33). Moreover, marriage between believers is sanctified in the context of exhortations more broadly concerned with distinguishing Christians from nonbelievers (see Eph. 4:17—5:20; 6:10-20). ...[3]

As stated above, today most biblical scholars agree that Ephesians is not authentic Paul. However, a huge portion of Christians still believe Paul to be its author. Consequently, for their sake, I shall now examine the Greek in a few controversial verses pertaining to women. Pointing out which passages were not written by Paul according to biblical scholars should be enough, but the hierarchal relationship between husband and wife in some forgeries is made even more hierarchal by the Aristotelian mindset of seventeenth-century English Christian translators.

Let's begin by examining a passage that was put through the Aristotelian blender and run through the grinder, altering the original meaning. The passage is Ephesians 5:20-25, 31, 33:

20 Giving thanks always for all things unto God and the Father in the name of our Lord Jesus Christ;

21 Submitting yourselves one to another in the fear of God.

22 Wives, submit yourselves unto your own husbands, as unto the Lord.

23 For the husband is the head of the wife, even as Christ is the head of the church: and he is the saviour of the body.

24 Therefore as the church is subject unto Christ, so let the wives be to their own husbands in every thing.

25 Husbands, love your wives, even as Christ also loved the church, and gave himself for it;

31 For this cause shall a man leave his father and mother, and shall be joined unto his wife, and they two shall be one flesh.

33 Nevertheless let every one of you in particular so love his wife even as himself; and the wife see that she reverence her husband.

Wow! Okay, where to begin to unravel the original teaching from the Aristotelian translation! I guess we will just start verse by verse, uncovering the problems in the translations and retranslating according to the original author's post-Pauline message.

## Submitting yourselves/Submit yourselves

In verse 21, both men and women are asked to submit themselves to one another for the good of the cause, the Church. Even in English there is no suggestion in the submitting that one is being *commanded* to *obey*. It is non-sexual love among church members serving in one accord, and the Greek verb is in the non-imperative (not commanding) mood.

Also in verse 21 is implied the Church's submitting itself voluntarily to Christ in brotherly and sisterly love and devotion. Drs. Osiek, MacDonald, and Tulloch have already pointed out above how in Paul's day the feminine relationship was with the community and Christ; here, the Church and Christ.

The problem comes up in verse 22: "Wives, submit yourselves unto your own husbands..." The connotation here in English is that wives are to obey their husbands. Yet the word for *submit* is not in the original Greek manuscript. It is supplied from the verse before where no *commanding* or *obeying* is implied, but a non-sexual partnership in Christ. The last part of verse 22, "as unto the Lord," shows that the writer was suggesting a voluntary joining of partners between husband and wife similar to that between the Church and Christ, a common theme after Paul's day.

Just looking at the vocabulary in this passage is not enough to understand it. The grammar must also be examined. Just relying upon the base word for *submit, hupotasso,* in Strong's, is misleading. In context, the word used is *hupotassomai,* which is present tense and shares reflective endings with both the passive and middle voices, the latter voice not occurring in English. If it is passive voice, it might be translated either, "Wives, ye are governed by your husbands" or "Wives, ye are subject to your husbands." Either is hierarchical but is not a command. The words simply state a fact or condition of the Greek culture, even at the end of the first century as the church moved from the feminine domain of house-churches to the masculine domain in the Greek public culture.

According to Dr. John Temple Bristow in his book *What Paul REALLY Said About Women,* the verb *submit* is in the Greek middle voice.[4] According to the *A Greek-English Lexicon,* the middle voice for the verb in question would translate "to make subject to oneself."[5] How do you translate *that* into English? A head-scratching, literal translation would be something like this: "Wives, make yourselves subject to yourselves for your husbands."

According to the "Greek Verbs Quick Reference" in *Greek Quick Reference Guide,* "[The middle voice] means that the SUBJECT initiates the action and participates in the results of the action. The middle voice indicates the subject performs an action upon himself or herself (reflexive action) or for their own benefit."[6] In an article dealing with New Testament Greek, we learn that "the Greek middle voice shows the <u>subject</u> acting in his own interest or on his own behalf, or participating in the results of the verbal action. In overly simplistic terms, sometimes the middle form of the verb could be translated as 'the performer of the action actually acting upon himself' (reflexive action)."[7]

In another source addressing the imperative mood in the Greek middle voice, the writer states that he believes two voices, active and passive, "are enough, and that's why the so-called *middle voice* has been trivialized in Modern Greek, to the point that only a single form exists in it, the *middle imperative.*"[8] But such was not the case in the first century. Back then, Greek had all the suffixes to indicate the voice and mood of the respective Greek forms. The writer of Ephesians did NOT use the Greek imperative mood when either addressing women or writing about them. He was NOT commanding women when he used *hupotassomai* or any of the other middle voice constructions of that verb. Instead, if this verb should be translated in the middle voice instead of the passive, he was requesting women to think through their relationship with their husbands and figure out a loving way to support these men in their service to Christ and the church.

Even in the middle voice the passage is somewhat hierarchical, although this patriarchal attitude is not as strong as with the passive voice and especially the active voice. Some think that since the verb *submit* does not appear in the Greek in verse 22 ("Wives, submit yourselves into your own husbands...") but is carried over from the previous verse, 21 ("Submitting yourselves one to another in the fear of God") and since it is not commanding nor stating necessarily an already established condition in verse 21 but a suggestion for good Christians to seriously consider, the verb should be translated from the middle voice in verse 21 (Submitting yourselves unto yourselves to determine how ye can best help one another in the love of God). Thus, if it is in the middle voice in verse 21, it should naturally be in the middle voice in verse 22 (Wives, subject yourselves unto yourselves to determine how ye can best help your husbands in serving Christ). Yes, still hierarchical, but more voluntary.

Let us examine the King James' translation of verse 22: "Wives, submit yourselves to your own husbands." This translation is neither passive voice nor middle. It is clearly active voice and appears as a command even though the Greek verb is in a non-imperative mood: subject ("Wives, [understood *ye*]") + verb ("submit") + direct object ("yourselves") + indirect object ("to your own husbands").

In some cases, it is permissible to translate the Greek middle voice into the English active. For example, take the sentence "The man washes himself." In ancient Greek, this verb *washes* would be in the middle voice because the man is doing something to benefit himself. This sense of benefit is carried over in the English active voice as expressed above.

But in other cases, the sense of the sentence subject's benefiting himself or herself is lost in the English active voice. It may have been appropriate to translate the middle voice in Ephesians 5:21

into English's active voice because the subject, the understood Christians, were all being benefited and the phrase comes across as a suggestion or recommendation rather than a command to meet the Greek's non-imperative mood. But in verse 22 when the verb is missing in the original Greek and is assumed to be the same as in verse 21, can the Greek verb for *submit*, in the middle voice, non-imperative mood, be accurately translated into the English active voice again? Only if the subject (*wives*, understood *ye*) receives some kind of benefit and the mood doesn't change into the imperative mood in the condition of a command.[9]

Examine verse 22 again: "Wives, submit yourselves to your own husbands" *KJV*; "Let women be subject to their husbands" *Douay Version*. What benefit is being accorded to the wives here except avoiding an ancient (and even present time) beating for being disobedient to the word of Aristotle disguised as the word of God? (In Afghanistan a few years ago, a twelve-year-old girl forced into marriage had her nose cut off by her husband. Yes, Christianity is not the only religion greatly influenced by Aristotle.) That is why *A Greek-English Lexicon* noted that the middle voice for *submit* should be translated "to make one subject to oneself." In this case, something like this: "Wives, make yourselves subject to yourselves for your husbands." The level of patriarchy here appears to be a bridge from the non-patriarchal apostolic church and the Aristotelian Christianity of the second century. The post-Pauline fathers appear to have influenced the English translators of Ephesians 5:22 in both the King James and Douay Versions. Thus, English-speaking Protestants and Catholics alike have been reshaped by the ancient pagan philosopher's views of women.

What would cause the seventeenth-century English translators of the Scriptures to adopt the active voice with imperative mood in English instead of the passive or middle voice with non-imperative mood from the Greek—when it came to dealing with women? It would appear that the translators who had adopted the pagan views of women from Aristotle, which had supplanted Christ's even before Aristotle's were Christianized in the thirteenth century, had no problem translating the Ephesians author's middle voice as active. They even may not have been consciously aware of how their ancient Greek views of women influenced their translation.

There are very few languages on earth that have a middle voice. As non-Pauline epistles have been translated into other languages without this middle voice, could the patriarchic translators for those languages have used the active voice in translating the Greek passive or middle voice of *hupotassomai,* thus corrupting the message about women in various languages around the globe as some have done in English?

Since more and more biblical scholars are agreeing that Paul did not write the epistle to the Ephesians, why even be concerned about the verb *hupotassomai?* Yes, Paul had died a few decades before; no matter whether it is active, passive, or middle voice, the attitude here is hierarchical—women are subject to men—according to this ancient writer. The point is that Aristotelian Christianity had apparently influenced the English translators—and still some today—to mistranslate the voice of the verb to conform more with Aristotle's views of women—a more potent statement—and insist that Aristotle's word is Paul's word.

It is the duty of a translator, when faced with a grammatical structure that does not translate, to vary from the literal words being translated to ones that best convey the thought of the original writer. Of all the Bibles I have examined, I think the best non-Aristotelian interpretation of Ephesians 5:22 is that by Dr. Eugene H. Peterson in his *The Message: The Bible in Contemporary Language*: "Wives, understand and support your husbands in ways that show your support for Christ." Aristotle has been filtered out, although I must admit that in the original there is some pagan contamination in that otherwise beloved epistle.

A PBS program says that all three monotheistic religions—Judaism, Christianity, and Islam—teach men and women to "love a spouse the way God loves us."[10] However, today an examination of actuality shows that some men don't necessarily follow this teaching. Patriarchy contradicts all three faiths, substituting Aristotle's commanding and obeying for loving. Many domineering men think, and even say, that they love their wife, but their love is often not the same as that taught by Christ Jesus or Paul. Likewise, in Christianity, when it comes to dealing with women, most translators have been influenced by Patriarchy more than by Christ's Christianity.

## Translation of *Head*

In English, when one hears the word *head*, one may picture a boss, a ruler, or a leader of some group or organization. But one may also picture that body part attached atop the neck. But in Greek, separate words distinguish the boss from the body part.

According to Strong's, *archon* is usually translated as *chief ruler, magistrate, prince, ruler*. It is used where one person has authority and another is expected to obey. The other Greek word that can be translated *head* is *kephale*, which is the body part. In Greek, this word never implies any kind of authority[11] where, as Aristotle taught, men were better fit to command and women to obey. But when this word is translated into English, the implication rings of authority, which, if translated back into Greek, would be *archon*. If *kephale* is translated as *leader*, it does NOT mean *ruler* or *one giving commands* but instead one out front first in the battle leading the charge,[12] as Jesus Christ did in paving the way by example. He is sometimes called the Exemplar.

The writer of Ephesians wrote of the members of the Church as all being the members of one body with Christ as the head (*kephale*) leading the Church by example rather than by commands or orders. Likewise, the writer taught that the husband was the head (*kephale*) of his family, leading his wife by example, not authority. If this head began acting like *archon* instead of *kephale*, then it was the wife's loving duty to serve as the neck to turn the head back to its natural Christian state of *kephale*, to serve in the family as the same *kephale* example that Jesus Christ had done for his body, the Church. In the following passage (Ephesians 5:22-25) in *The Message Bible*, note how the translator avoided any possible Aristotelian interpretation of *head* by not even using the word:

> Wives, understand and support your husbands in ways that show your support for Christ. The husband provides leadership [from *kephale*] to his wife the way Christ does to his church, not by domineering but by cherishing. So just as the church submits to Christ as he exercises such leadership, wives should likewise submit to their husbands.

Remember, as this translator has done with the first verse here, that *submit* at the end also would appear to be the Greek middle voice, "make yourselves subject to yourselves." Examine your purpose in life, in the church, in the home, and join your husbands in serving Christ. There is no hint of commanding wives to obey their husbands. As a matter of fact, a condition for following is implied: Follow the husband as he "submits to Christ as he exercises such leadership [from *kephale*] ...." The focus is on self-examination and Christian mission. Retire, Aristotle!

Before leaving Ephesians 5, we should examine another thought. For centuries, Ephesians 5 and other passages have been used to confirm with Christian women that they are commanded to submit to their husbands in bed. Paul never commanded such, and the writer of Ephesians 5 did not either. Paul never commanded sexual desire or love (*eros*). In Greek mythology, Eros was the god of love, son of Aphrodite, goddess of love. He was the Greek equivalent of the later Roman Cupid. Although Paul did not promote erotic love, he did say that "it is better to marry than to burn" (I Corinthians 7:9). He himself adhered to continence and thought it well if others did, also. He furthermore cautioned not to "defraud" one's mate by withholding sex unless the abstinence is by mutual consent and for a short time, accompanied with "fasting and prayer" so that neither is tempted outside the marriage during this period. Also implied under defrauding is withholding sex as a punishment to one's mate. See I Corinthians 7:2-5.

In Ephesians 5, the writer used what many Christians consider a higher form of love, *agapao*, a term becoming more and more popular today.[13] It is the same word John used when he declared, "God is love" (I John 4:8). Note how the writer described this love between a husband and wife in the remaining verses of Ephesians 5. Like his Master, the writer also referred to Genesis 2:24: "Therefore shall a man leave his father and his mother, and shall cleave unto his wife: and they shall be one flesh." They are one in love with each other, just as part of the Church, they are one, in love, with Christ, the head of the Church. Enjoy *The Message Bible's* rendition of these verses:

> Husbands, go all out in your love for your wives, exactly as Christ did for the church—a love marked by giving, not getting. Christ's love makes the church whole. His words evoke her beauty. Everything he does and says is designed to bring the best out of her, dressing her in dazzling white silk, radiant with holiness. And that is how husbands ought to love their wives. They're really doing themselves a favor— since they're already "one" in marriage.

No one abuses his own body, does he? No, he feeds and pampers it. That's how Christ treats us, the church, since we are part of his body. And this is why a man leaves father and mother and cherishes his wife. No longer two, they become "one flesh." This is a huge mystery, and I don't pretend to understand it all. What is clearest to me is the way Christ treats the church. And this provides a good picture of how each husband is to treat his wife, loving himself in loving her, and how each wife is to honor her husband.

Aristotle is subordinated to Christ to the extent that the Greek philosopher vanishes.

But the Aristotelian *head* emerges over and over again with its sadistic grin. Take I Corinthians 11:3: "But I would have you know, that the head of every man is Christ; and the head of the woman is the man; and the head of Christ is God." Here we have the same problem with *head* as we did in Ephesians 5. Both uses of *head* come to mind in English: (1) one who exercises authority (*archon*) and (2) the head (skull, etc.) of the body, where any sense of leadership does not imply authority but instead one who is out first in battle setting an example (*kephale*). Paul used this second word of *head*, but when it is translated into English, we also assume the first Greek word for *head*. Thus the translation of *kephale* into English as *head* is misleading, to say the least. It implies the Aristotelian opposite of what Paul taught. The problem is most translations of the Bible follow the King James and Douay use of *head*, implying a falsehood. One Bible uses *responsible to*, but that rings more of *archon* than Paul's *kephale*. One substituted *authority* for *head*, a clear variation from Paul's thought.

The challenge is finding a clear translation of *kephale* for English that is in accord with Paul's teaching: "There is neither male nor female: for ye are all one in Christ Jesus" (Galatians 3:28). Borrowing the term *support* from *The Message Bible* in Ephesians 5 and using part of the definition of *kephale*, we might consider something like this: "But I would have you know, that the support and example for every man is Christ; and the support and example for the wife is the husband; and the support for Christ is God." That is not to deny that God may have authority over Christ and Christ over man, but that simply is not what Paul was writing about in this verse, not with the word *kephale* instead of *archon*.

My daughter, a schoolteacher, after reading the above, said, "But women look to Christ, too. A woman doesn't have to go through a husband to find Christ." I agreed, because as quoted above, Paul wrote, "There is neither male nor female: for ye are all one in Christ Jesus" (Galatians 3:28). But we must also acknowledge the challenge Paul had in building a Church from two cultures, Hebrew and Greek, both of which were based on hard-core dominance by men. Also, Paul had to proceed cautiously because of Augustus Caesar's Marriage Laws. All non-military men up to the age of 60 and all women up to 50 (including widows) had to marry and have children. Those unmarried would lose their inheritance. The fewer the children a couple had among the elite, the more taxes the couple had to pay. Once a woman had three children, she was free of her husband's authority without divorcing him.[14] And we must remember that Roman law did not have a state attorney to prosecute crimes; any citizen could place charges and have another arrested and brought to court. We saw this happen to Paul those times when he was stoned and put into prison. Since his epistles were to be read aloud in the churches as though he were there preaching and since, if any member who had withdrawn his membership from the church, could bring charges against Paul and the Church because he preached the emancipation of women before they had three children, Paul had to word his letters most cautiously. Likewise, the author of Ephesians, when writing about *submitting*, instead of using the active voice, as was used in the Latin Roman laws, had to choose his words cautiously, using the Greek middle voice, making the submitting voluntary, having the women submit themselves to themselves to find the best way to support their husband in the same way they both would support Christ for the sake of the Church. It's not as though a woman needs to look to her husband to find Christ, but rather through Christ she can support her husband, distinct from the idea that a woman was only to obey her husband.

Furthermore, if a woman could support herself (a rare situation in those days) and not depend upon a man and avoid prosecution under Augustus Caesar's Marriage Laws for not being married and having children, she could go directly to Christ without affecting a man's ego. Paul even favored, but not required, a non-marital life. But Paul, being a Roman citizen and not being married, again had to choose his words carefully.

In addition, as we can see from the many examples at the end of this chapter, Paul named many women who were leaders in his churches. He even honored a married couple, Priscilla and Aquilla, mentioning *her* name first, a sign that she probably was the greater of the two in Christ's work. One of the important things a Christian woman today must consider before marrying is the ego and stability of the man. One cannot marry, hoping the spouse will change. She must ask herself beforehand, will he dominate her or treat her as being inferior, or will this be a union where two individuals can grow together without jealousy and condemnation, "for ye are all one in Christ Jesus"?

Further down in I Corinthians 11, we come to verse 13: "Judge in yourselves: is it comely that a woman pray unto God uncovered?" Paul may have been concerned with Greek culture here. Remember that church services were held in a member's house. Some neighbors were curious why people were visiting a neighbor on a regular basis. Telescopic eyeballs connected with imagination and probably widened during those sessions of "interpretation of tongues." At least in a few cases, big ears thought they were hearing the signs of sexual orgy. Christian reputations needed preserving. But Thomas Aquinas used this passage as one to justify not ordaining women as priests.[15] The reasoning? She must keep her long hair and not have a patch shaved off the crown of her head. A priest had to have a shaved patch on the crown, called a tonsure. According to Aquinas' requirements, Christ Jesus himself, his apostles, and Paul with their hair would not have been described as priests in Aquinas' concept of church.

## Timothy 2:11, 12

Let's look at another passage, mainly because it is one of two that Aquinas used to declare that women could not be ordained as priests. Most biblical scholars today have concluded that Paul's epistles to Timothy and the one to Titus were not actually written by Paul. It was customary even back with the Hebrews and later in the early Christian church *beyond* Paul's day to ascribe one's writings to a widely known individual in order to get one's own views recognized. The message was more of concern to these writers than the credit for the ideas. Today such an act would be considered dishonest, even deceptive. But apparently not so in ancient times. Dr. Bristow offers several reasons why these epistles were not written by Paul:

- "The churches described in these letters seem to be highly organized, more so than one would expect to find during the lifetime of the apostles."[16] He cites examples from I Timothy 3:1-13; 5:1-19 and Titus 1:5-16. There is no evidence, for example, that Paul's little churches, which met in members' homes with voluntary services, ever paid salaries to the elders.
- The office of bishop (see I Timothy 3) was formed after the apostolic age.
- The Greek style and vocabulary of these three epistles are different than Paul's writings. "And more than one-third of the words in these epistles (excluding names) are used nowhere else in Paul's writings."[17]
- The attitude toward women in I Timothy 2:11-13 is vastly different from that found in Paul's writings. And, I might add, distinct from what Jesus taught. A note in *The Interpretive Bible* states: "Obviously the disposition of this epistle to limit the service of women in the churches does not accord with Jesus' attitude of complete respect and chivalry toward women."[18]
- Then there are the apparent attacks against Gnostic Christianity. I might add that, in addition to Dr. Bristow's discussion here, I Timothy 2 appears be more from that post-apostolic church, the growing patriarchic church concerned about the high position of women in the Gnostic church. Note that Gnostic Christianity promoted Mary Magdalene at the expense of Simon Peter, the champion advanced by the patriarchic church.[19]
- The writer of Ephesians near the end of the first century wrote in chapter 2 verses 8 and 9 that "by grace you are saved through faith...not because of works, lest any man should boast."[20] But in I Timothy 2, after attacking the position of women in the church, this writer wrote that a woman "shall be saved in childbearing..." (verse 15). Such a notion certainly came not only *after* Paul's time, but also after the time of the writer of Ephesians—during the patriarchic church's treatment of women.
- This writer presented Adam and Eve in a way that is the exact opposite of Paul's thought, as we shall see shortly. Here in I Timothy 2:13, 14, this writer penned: "13 For Adam was first formed, then Eve. 14 And Adam was not deceived,

but the woman being deceived was in the transgression." What a contrast to I Corinthians 11:11, 12, which, as I said, we will cover shortly. Furthermore, I Timothy's reference to Adam and Eve puts all the blame for the fall from grace on Eve. But in I Corinthians 15, Paul focused on Adam: "22 For as in Adam all die, even so in Christ shall all be made alive. 45 And so it is written, The first man Adam was made a living soul; the last Adam [the Christ] was made a quickening spirit."

- I wish to add another factor to Pastor Bristow's list. A note in *The Interpreter's Bible* about I Timothy 2 reads, "In regard to the place of women in church, the writer has reverted toward the older Jewish practice. In part this may have been caused by extravagances [perhaps in clothing or jewelry, or chitchatting in church] resulting from the primitive Christian 'emancipation' of women, in part by a natural masculine reluctance to yield historic prerogatives to women."[21] This second reason mentioned at the very end, although it gets the point across about "masculine reluctance," is a pleasant euphemism for "patriarchic tendencies." Such tendencies, however, were not characteristic of Paul; as a matter of fact, they were contrary to his teachings. Such tendencies *were* characteristic of the writers of the post-apostolic, patriarchic church of the second century and beyond.

Although Dr. Bristow does not believe that the Pastoral epistles (I and II Timothy and Titus) were written by Paul, he does allow for that possibility. Dr. Ehrman states outright that these are "pseudonymous writings," meaning that the writer was not Paul but one using his name.[22] Also, Dr. Luke T. Johnson, professor of New Testament and Christian Origins at Emory University, writes that the Pastoral epistles "are certainly pseudonymous."[23] Dr. Bristow's allowing for the possibility that the Pastoral epistles could be authentic appears to be only his addressing the doubts of some unscholarly Christians that these epistles really could be forgeries.

Now let us examine the two main verses in I Timothy 2 that are in question:

11 Let the woman learn in silence with all subjection.

12 But I suffer not a woman to teach, nor to usurp
authority over the man, but to be in silence.

In verse 11, the word for *silence* is *hesuchia*, which, according
to Strong's, focuses on *stillness, not bustling, quietness*. The word
*subjection*, according to Strong's and Bristow, comes from the word
for *to submit*. One friend who knows Greek better than I said that
this nominal form of *huputassô* may be "built on the active form of
the verb." If so, the voluntary concept of the middle voice disappears
and Aristotle's word of obedience is preached as the word of God.
The hierarchical nature of ancient pagan Grecian culture is well
embedded in Christianity by the second century.

Also, verse 12 begins so untypical of Paul. Of course, as the
church started, the women could not teach or preach outside of
leading prayer, prophesying, or speaking in tongues because they
simply were not educated. Those coming out of Judaism certainly
were uneducated, and the only Greek educated women were
prostitutes, who would attract men with educated conversations.
The implication is that Greek men found educated women sexy. But
the point is there were simply no or few Christian educated women
when the church first began to be asked to teach. But the tone and
style of "I suffer or permit or allow not a woman to teach" does not
sound like Paul. He taught that men should follow Jesus' example of
leading by example, not commanding women and expecting them to
obey. As discussed before, such commanding is contrary to Paul's
expression of love, *agapao*. Consequently, the writer here does *not*
appear to be reflecting on the teaching situation of the apostolic
church but instead expressing the bias of the later second-century
patriarchic church.

The next part of verse 12, as translated here, certainly is a
patriarchic expression: "nor to usurp authority over the man."
The word for *authority, authenteô*, is its only use in the Bible
and according to *The Interpreter's Bible* "is obscure." It has been
translated "interrupt" and "dictate to."[24] We might add "dominate"
and "domineer." Take your pick: they all sound negative, lacking
*agapao*, ringing of masculine domination, contrary to Jesus and
Paul's teaching of equality in the apostolic church. But keep in
mind that the most common meaning of this present infinitive form
of this verb is "to have full power or authority over"—clearly the
boiling blood of Aristotle from a Christian quill.

The *silence* at the end of the verse is *hesuchia*, just as in the previous verse, *stillness, not bustling, quietness,* the only favorable note in verse 12.

It is this verse 12 that Aquinas used to support his claim that women should not be ordained as priests.[25] The patriarchy of Aquinas's thirteenth century reached back to the patriarchy of the second century claiming to be Paul's patriarchy to justify a limited position for women in the church.

The Aristotelian, or ancient Greek, patriarchy is embedded this time in the original script. The translation may add to it, but it is different in this case because the original Greek script is the filter itself for the beginning of the patriarchy to replace the teaching of Jesus, Paul, and the apostolic church. *The Message Bible* can remove the patriarchic filter in the translation, but the eyes of Aristotle can still be seen peeking through the thoughts of the original Greek words: "I don't let women take over and tell men what to do. They should study to be quiet and obedient along with everyone else."

It is right after these verses that the writer of I Timothy launches into "the transgression" of Eve and how a woman "shall be saved in childbearing." But what about those women who couldn't have children because of problems with either her or her husband? Faith, as both Paul and the writer of Ephesians taught, would apparently not be sufficient to save her, although her husband, even if he were the one with the physical difficulty, could be saved because he is a man. And what about Paul's preference for abstinence? A woman cannot be abstinent and also have a baby! Certainly this writer cannot be proposing that women should all become Virgin Marys! This Scriptural quote is so ridiculous, so contrary to Paul's teaching, more like the children requirement of Augustus Caesar's Marriage Laws, that we should move on.

# Titus 2:3-5

Most biblical scholars are agreed that Paul did not write Titus. Another Aristotelian interpretation falsely ascribed to Paul can be found in Titus 2:3-5, where we find the phrase "obedient to their own husbands":

3 The aged women ... be in behavior as becometh holiness, not false accusers, not given to much wine, teachers of good things;

4 That they may teach the young women to be sober, to love their husbands, to love their children,

5 To be discreet, chaste, keepers at home, good, obedient to their own husbands, that the word of God be not blasphemed.

The adjective *obedient* is a translation from the same Greek verb used back in Ephesians 5, *submit*, except that, as with the word *subjection* in I Timothy, this second-century author claiming to be Paul used the active voice. Thus, as in I Timothy, any voluntary implications that come with the middle voice are non-existent.

## I Corinthians 14:34, 35

The reader may remember that back in Chapter 3 Aristotle was quoted quoting the Greek poet Sophocles: "Silence is a woman's glory." This view had become a part of patriarchal Christianity long before Thomas Aquinas had Christianized Aristotle. Contrary to Paul's teaching, women later were not to preach, prophesy, or speak in church. So it was only natural for those men translating the New Testament into English to think a silent woman was a sacred teaching dating back to the beginning of Christianity. Such is far from the truth, although one would hardly know that from reading most English translations.

For example, take I Corinthians 14:34, 35:

34 Let your women keep silence in the churches: for it is not permitted unto them to speak; but they are commanded to be under obedience, as also saith the law.

35 And if they will learn any thing, let them ask their husbands at home: for it is a shame for women to speak in the church.

Biblical scholars are agreed that Paul wrote I Corinthians and are also generally agreed that verses 34 and 35 of chapter 14 were added decades after Paul was martyred. One of the first things that catch the eye of scholars is that these two verses sometimes appear as 34 and 35 in some Bibles and at the end of chapter 14 in others. In his book on I Corinthians, Dr. Gordon D. Fee writes that

> one must assume that the words were first written as a gloss in the margin by someone who, probably in light of 1 Tim. 2:9-15, felt the need to qualify Paul's instructions even further. Since the phenomenon of glosses making their way into the biblical text is so well documented elsewhere in the NT (e.g., John 5:3b-4; 1 John 5:7), there is no good historical reason to reject the possibility here.[26]

Since I Corinthians 14:34, 35 is written in the same second-century vein as I Timothy, which, as already shown, is a forgery produced long after Paul and his apostolic church, then these two verses in I Corinthians lend themselves to being a forgery, also. If Fee is right, that these two verses were written to further "Paul's" instructions in I Timothy, then these two verses were penned even later in the second century. We probably will never know exactly what happened, except that the marginal gloss was inserted in two different places by different scribes, or biblical copyists. None of the original manuscripts exists, only copies made from copies made from copies.

Dr. Fee offers more explanations why verses 34 and 35 are not authentic. He writes: "Various reasons have been given for the gloss, all relating to the known situation of the church at the end of the first century or the beginning of the second (e.g., the attempt to check a rising feminist movement [cf. 1 Tim. 2:9-15; 5:11-15]; to reconcile 1 Cor.14 with 1 Tim. 2)."[27]

Let us focus a moment on this last point, "to reconcile 1 Cor. 14 with 1 Tim. 2." Chapter 11 of I Corinthians obviously contradicts I Timothy and these two verses intended to reconcile I Corinthians with I Timothy. Fee points out the great difficulty of reconciling these verses with "11:2-16, where it is assumed without reproof that women pray and prophesy in the assembly, not to mention that such is also assumed in the repeated 'all' of vv. 23-24 and 31 and the 'each one' of v. 26."[28]

The Scofield Bible notes that the word *pneumatika* ("matters of or from the Holy Spirit") gives the key to chapters 12, 13, and 14. "Chapter 12 concerns the Spirit in relation to the body of Christ. ... Chapter 13 continues the *pneumatika* begun in chapter 12. Gifts are good, but only if ministered in love." Chapter 14 is still on the subject of *pneumatika*, focusing on the importance of prophesying because it "edifieth the church" (verse 4).[29] Paul had already established in chapter 11 that women pray and prophesy in the assembly, so why would he in the middle of a chapter devoted to prophesying in church suddenly in verses 34 and 35 say that "women keep silence in the churches," that "it is not permitted unto them to speak," that "it is a shame for women to speak in the church"? The writer here, especially with that argument about *shame*, is voicing the ideas of some Christian men in the second century, ideas adopted from ancient Greek culture that it is shameful for women to speak in a public place. By the second century, the church was moving out of private homes into public buildings. Paul was following his Master's example to free women, but in the second century, ancient pagan views about women were taking over in church doctrine.

Read chapter 14 on prophecy in light of what Paul wrote about women prophesying in chapter 11. Note how out of place verses 34 and 35 are. Now take out those verses. Note how the chapter becomes a continuous discourse and reads much better.

There may still be some readers who are not yet convinced that these two verses are forgeries. So, to help these readers, although I agree with Dr. Fee, I will examine here the Greek of 14:34, 35 as though it is authentic Paul. However, I will be referring to the author of these two verses as *the writer*.

According to Strong's, the Greek word for *silence* is *sigao*. It comes from *sige*, which is a voluntary refusal to speak. Paul used this *sigao* six verses before when he cautioned those who spoke in tongues to "keep silence in the church" "if there be no interpreter." Such a person (man or woman) was not being told never to speak in church but do so when all have a chance of understanding so as to avoid tumult.

According to *A Greek-English Lexicon*, an alternate form of *sigao* (*silence*) means the opposite of *talkative*. This would suggest that part of the tumult the writer was concerned about was being caused by some talkative women speaking either out of turn or chitchatting when they should be listening. The writer was requesting them to keep order by speaking only in turn. Some verses before, Paul had encouraged them to pray and prophesy in church, not never to speak, and here the writer in the Greek appears to be in agreement.

The reader may also remember from my last chapter, the idea in verse 34 above, that women "are commanded to be under obedience," also came directly out of Aristotle and ruled the Greek culture of Paul's day although the apostle opposed its use in the church; Aristotle wrote that "the courage of man is shown in commanding, of a woman in obeying," that "the temperance ... of a man is in commanding and of a woman is in obeying," that "the male is by nature fitter for command than the female," and that the male-female "inequality is permanent." These ideas may be sacred in patriarchal Christianity, but they have nothing to do with the teachings of either Jesus or Paul.

Note that in verse 34 above, the words "they [the women] are commanded" do not even appear in the Greek manuscripts. They were supplied by the patriarchic Christian translators who obviously were influenced by the Christianization of Aristotle's diabolical views of women. Furthermore, note that the words "to be under obedience" are an Aristotelian mistranslation perhaps made to have this gloss agree with Titus 2:4, 5. The word used here is the same as in Ephesians: *hupotassomai*, in the middle voice meaning, "to make subject to oneself." In other words, women, make yourselves subject unto yourselves. That is, examine what you are doing and, when tempted to chitchat or speak out of turn, control yourselves; otherwise, you are contributing to the tumult needed to be cleared up in the Corinthian church. What a difference when we remove the Aristotelian translation filter!

The word *speak* appears twice in this English translation of I Corinthians 14:34, 35 (KJV). Pastor Bristow notes that "Greek has many words that can be translated 'speak.' Five of them denote preaching or proclaiming, and twenty-five others can be translated 'say,' 'speak,' or 'teach.'"[30] The word the writer used in both cases is *laleo*. Dr. Bristow points out that only this verb of the 25 can also mean, simply, "talk."[31] As a matter of fact, Strong's gives the chief meaning as *to talk*. A *Greek-English Lexicon* gives the chief meaning as *to talk, chat, babble, prattle*. Another definition is *to chatter*. Chatting, babbling, prattling, and chattering all indicate the kind of talking the women should not have been doing in church. What was shameful was chatting during prayer or while someone else was speaking. The writer of these two verses was calling for women to stop inappropriate talking during church. He was not forbidding them to speak or prophesy or lead prayer in church. The same translators who had added the words that women "were commanded" and mistranslated self-examination as "obedience" again went with a slant of words appearing to say that women were never to speak in church.

Several times in the past I have attended women's business conferences, not as an attendee, but as a helper, one of several men available to move furniture on stage or run errands. I remember that at the first of these, there was a woman up front giving instructions to all the groups into which the women were divided, while at the same time the women at the head of each group circle were also speaking, and while at the same time all the women were talking with the women with whom they had been paired. To me, being a member of the male species, I thought I was witnessing utter chaos! Even the men in the British House of Commons don't produce this much tumult! But at the end of the women's session, all the women were pleased as to how well things went, how much they had learned, even grateful that they had experienced more than they had expected! I was both amazed and confused! To me, it was a case of the Big Bang somehow evolving into order and cohesion.

If I am on the phone and my wife tries to tell me something, instinctively my other hand goes up to wave her off because I can't listen to two people speaking at the same time. So does that mean that I cannot multitask or change between tasks quickly?

Studies show that there is no significant difference in productivity between the sexes while multitasking. However, although both sexes had drops in IQ after multitasking, the men's loss in IQ was significantly higher than the women's.[32] This loss may explain why in another study, women were significantly more accurate than men while multitasking.[33] A British study may explain this greater loss in IQ and in accuracy for men: While multitasking, "men tended to start their search in a less logical place such as the centre of the field and they would not cover the whole area when they were outlining their search. Women tended to enter in one corner and search in concentric circles or lines."[34] Women with children also are forced to practice their multitasking skills.

A friend told me of a woman who at the same time could breast-feed her infant, cook dinner, talk with a friend on the phone, and, using her big toe, text her husband to let him know when dinner was going to be ready. I asked whether this was a bit exaggerated and was told "yea" as long as I put the emphasis on "a bit."

"You mean the 'big toe' part?" I asked. The answer was a grin.

Big toe or no big toe, how can women do it? Apparently, because women have more practice, especially those with several children. Men aren't as often forced into such circumstances, and those men like me who are focused on details and accuracy tend to steer away from anything that might diminish accuracy, even if more productivity rather than accuracy is desirable at times.

In any case, men and women obviously communicate differently. Now try putting these men and women in a church service together where the women are communicating naturally for women, chitchatting, talking, and asking questions of their husbands, who probably are like me: they cannot talk and listen to their wives and the speaker at the same time. For the men, this kind of service would be utter chaos, or tumult, to use the writer's term. The writer wanted to keep the men in the fold. Apparently, he had received reports of such chaos—obviously reported by men. To keep the men, the writer requested that the women not chitchat or talk out of turn in church, including not asking their husbands questions, which would disrupt those around such a couple and disrupt the husband's one-track mind focused on the speaker. Women were still encouraged to prophesy and speak in church, but only one at a time when it was their individual turn to do so. It would appear that the writer knew of no other way to bring men and women together to worship, sing, and pray. Note: This writer *requested*, not *commanded*.

As a matter of fact, to be honest, I have met *men* who also could benefit from this advice on chitchatting and talking out of turn during meetings—or should I say that the people around such men would be benefited.

\* \* \*

Even before his conversion, Paul had a strong choleric personality. Today we might call it a type A personality, or if we have read Robert Rohm's book,[35] a type D, *D* standing for *drive* and *domineering*, among other things. Being a dedicated Jew, named after the first king of Israel, Saul drove himself to completely dominate Jesus' followers. After his conversion, he kept his drive, this time to spread the word of the Messiah and establish a Christian church, but he brought his male domineering trait under control with *agapao*, the love and understanding that he taught. As mentioned before, he took the name of Paul, meaning "a humble one."

A man who practices what he preaches is appealing to women. A man who controls the male domineering trait is appealing to women. A man who has a vision and the drive to achieve it but who also masters his own male domineering instinct is a man whom women find *very* appealing, especially when the domineering factor is replaced with love and understanding. Paul was a man whom women could most respectfully follow. He was the one leader of his time who could pull men and women together—a whole new idea of the ages—to form and spread a united church based on Christ's love, not Aristotle's commanding and obeying.

Paul also had to handle controversy from Jewish theology. In I Corinthians 11, Paul disarmed the Adam-better-than-Eve issue:

> 11 ...neither is the man without the woman, neither the woman without the man, in the Lord.

> 12 For as the woman is of the man, even so is man also by the woman; but all things of God.

After Paul and Silas left Syria to spread the word abroad, Paul preached to some women by a river outside Philippi. There Lydia, a well-to-do woman ("a seller of purple"), became Paul's first convert in Europe when he baptized her and her household (Acts 16:13-15). In Thessalonica, Paul and Silas converted many Greeks "and of the chief women not a few" (Acts 17:4). Then off to Berea, where "many of them believed; also of honourable women which were Greeks, and of men, not a few" (Acts 17:11, 12). After preaching from Mars' Hill in Athens, Paul found many "clave unto him"; Paul mentioned two, one a woman named Damaris (Acts 17:34). After his church was established in Philippi, Paul wrote his followers there. He encouraged two women, Euodias and Syntyche, who apparently had some difference of opinions on some matter, to "be of the same mind in the Lord." He entreated his followers to "help those women which laboured with me in the gospel" (Philippians 4:2, 3). Obviously the women in that church were important leaders.

In the last chapter of Romans, Paul mentions 26 persons, eight of whom were women. As mentioned earlier, included were Priscilla and Aquila, a married couple; but note that Paul mentioned her name first, indicating that she was the greater of two who were "my helpers in Christ Jesus." Most notable is that in the beginning of Paul's close to the Romans (chapter 16), he allots two full verses to introducing Phebe:

> 1 I commend unto you Phebe our sister, which is a servant of the church which is at Cenchrea:
>
> 2 That ye receive her in the Lord, as becometh saints, and that ye assist her in whatever business she hath need of you: for she hath been a succourer of many, and of myself also.

Paul asked the Roman church to receive Phebe as though she were a saint. He referred to her as "a *succourer* of many, and of myself also." The Greek word for *succourer* is *prostatis* (the feminine form derived of *proistemi*) which, according to Strong's, would mean, one "*to stand before*, i.e., (in rank) *to preside*" and according to *A Greek-English Lexicon*, one who stands first in rank, a chief.[36] Where Phebe is referred to as "a servant of the church," the Greek word for *servant* is *diakonos*, which can mean *servant*, but, more importantly, *teacher, pastor, deacon, minister*. Pastor John Bristow in his book called her "a deacon of the church in Cenchreae."[37] Can you, dear reader, guess why the Aristotelian Christian translators went with *servant* instead of *deacon*?

When it comes to reading about women in the New Testament, one cannot always take as gospel the words on the printed page because they may be forgeries or may be tainted unconsciously by the Aristotelian mind-set of the translators. This mind-set has often automatically been reproduced in newer translations without closer examination. What we thought was the sacred word about women can be the opposite of what really is sacred. The word of Aristotle is often translated as the word of God. Then men become deceived and women subjugated in a patriarchic church. The so-called word of God concerning women then permeates Western culture.

The lies of Shakespeare's Iago once deceived and irrationally moved Othello on the world's stage into smothering the innocent life of Desdemona. The lies of Aristotle's patriarchy have deceived the church and much of the world's culture into still smothering the feminine half of humanity. Only the Truth can resurrect the bride.

# Endnotes
## Chapter 4

1  Margaret Y. MacDonald, *Early Christian Women and Pagan Opinion*, Cambridge, England: Cambridge University Press, 1996, pp. 30-31.
2  Bart D. Ehrman, *Forged*, New York: HarperOne, 2011, pp. 109-111.
3  Carolyn Osiek, Margaret Y. MacDonald, and Janet H. Tulloch, *A Woman's Place: House Churches in Earliest Christianity*, Minneapolis: Fortress Press, 2006, pp. 124-125.
4  John Temple Bristow, *What Paul REALLY Said About Women: An Apostle's Liberating Views on Equality in Marriage, Leadership, and Love*, HarperSanFrancisco, 1991, pp. 38-41.
5  *A Greek-English Lexicon*, 8th ed., comp. by Henry G. Liddell and Robert Scott, New York: American Book Co., 1897, p. 1640.
6  http://www.preceptaustin.org/new_page_40.htm, p. 6.
7  http://www.ntgreek.org/learn_nt_greek/verbs.htm, p. 2.
8  http://www.foundalis.com/lan/grkverbs.htm, p. 7.
9  It is worth noting that there was no verb in Ephesians 5:22 in many Greek manuscripts, such as the Greek Westcott and Holt Bible of the nineteenth century nor in the Tischendorf-Greek manuscript on which the Westcott and Holt was partially based. For the English, the verb had to be reckoned from verse 21, assuming that the Greek writer, as custom was, had so intended. Since the verb *submitting* in verse 21 is present tense, then the inferred verb for verse 22 also has to be present tense, which means that it can be translated as either passive or middle voice. But since the action in verse 21 is voluntary, offering a benefit or blessing to those who submit themselves to one another in the brotherhood and sisterhood of Christ, then such a middle voice attitude should appear in the reckoned meaning in verse 22.

In some Greek manuscripts copied from the more originals, the copyist took on what he thought was his duty to do the reckoning himself in the Greek manuscript itself that he was reproducing. For example, in the Greek manuscript Textus Receptus, from which the King James Version was translated, the verb *submit* reckoned from Ephesians 5: 21 for verse 22 appears in the Greek verse 22 itself. Consequently, the translators using this Greek manuscript may not have had cause to study the middle-voice implications in verse 21. Whoever supplied the reckoned verb from 21 for 22 in the Greek manuscript itself may have put the English translators of the King James at a disadvantage.

10 "Three Faiths, One God: Judaism, Christianity, Islam, Part I," PBS DVD, 2002.

11 Bristow, p. 36.

12 *Ibid.*, pp. 36-37.

13 This term *agapao* has been thought to be a higher form of love by Christians since the 1970's. Even though some Greek writers of the first century used it, however rarely, for sexual love, it is not so used in the New Testament.

14 Will Durant, *Caesar and Christ*, New York: Simon and Schuster, 1944, pp. 222-224.

15 Thomas Aquinas, *Summa Theologica*, Pt. III Supplement, ques. 39, art.1, trans. by Fathers of the English Dominican Province, London: Burns, Oates & Washbourne, 1915-1922.

16 Bristow, p. 67.

17 *Ibid.*

18 *The Interpreter's Bible*, vol. XI of XII, New York: Abingdon-Cokesbury Press, 1952, p. 406, note.

19 See Gnostic gospel in Karen L. King's *The Gospel of Mary of Magadala: Jesus and the First Woman Apostle*, Santa Rosa: Polebridge Press, 2003.

20 Not King James Version translation.

21 *The Interpreter's Bible*, vol. XI, p. 405.

22 See Dr. Ehrman's scholarly book, *The Orthodox Corruption of Scripture: The Effect of Early Christological Controversies on the Text of the New Testament*, paperback ed., New York: Oxford University Press, 1993, p. 33, endnote 11.

23 See Dr. Johnson's *The Apostle Paul*, a course guidebook, Chantilly, Virginia: The Teaching Company, 2001, p. 9.

24 *The Interpreter's Bible*, vol. XI, p. 405.

25 Aquinas, *Summa Theologica*, part. III Supplement, ques. 39, art.1.

26 Gordon D. Fee, *The First Epistle to the Corinthians*, Grand Rapids: William B. Eerdmans Publishing Co., 1987.

27 *Ibid.*, p. 699. See ftnt.

28 *Ibid.*, p. 702.

29 C. I. Scofield, *The Scofield Reference Bible*, New York: Oxford University Press, 1945, pp. 1222, 1223. See ftnts.

30 Bristow, p. 63.

31 *Ibid.*

32 http://clearinghouse.missouriwestern.edu/manuscripts/815. php, p. 3.

33 *Ibid.*, p. 4.

34 http://www.telegraph.co.uk/science/science-new/7896385/ Scientist-prove-that-women-are-better-at-multitasking-than-men, p. 2.

35 Robert A. Rohm, *Positive Personality Profiles*, Atlanta: Personality Insights, 1994.

36 *A Greek-English Lexicon*, p. 1321.

37 Bristow, p. 56.

# CHAPTER 5

## GOD: MASCULINE OR FEMININE OR BOTH? AND WHAT EFFECT THIS HAS ON OUR CONCEPT OF WOMEN

Since the status of women was embedded in religious beliefs and still is influenced by these beliefs, we cannot avoid discussing humankind's concept of God from which those beliefs evolved. Remember that theological concepts also were influenced by the position of women in society, the foundation of which was based on the ancient superstitions about their menstruation, on Greek philosophy, on the lack of Christians' following Jesus Christ's teaching and example concerning women, and on the mistranslations and forgeries of Paul's teaching about women. It has been an unbelievable merry-go-round ride with theology and superstitions and misunderstandings and ignorance and patriarchy and arrogance mounted on their statuette horses chasing weary women round and round through the millenniums. And if a woman decides to get off this ride, she often is treated like the helpless fox in a British hunt.

Since women were believed to be inferior and weak, then the whole gamut of feminine qualities, it was reasoned, could not be a significant, if any, part of omnipotence, or the Almighty. The cyclic reasoning would then conclude that since God is basically either only or mostly masculine, then women had a lesser place in His plan and purpose than He had for men.

Even languages, such as English, have evolved with no singular pronoun that endorses both the masculine and feminine. We have either *he* or *she*. The neuter *it* was not intended to combine *he* and *she* but to eliminate both. *They* can be the plural of either *he*, *she*, or *it*, or, depending upon the need, the combination of these. Some English scholars have suggested that *they* be considered singular as well as plural, but the linguistic purists are horrified at such a notion. Some writers have experimented with *s/he*. Most have resulted in either using *he or she* or writing mostly in the plural. These options, however, leave no singular pronoun in English to accommodate the growing concept of both the masculinity and femininity—the completeness—of an Elohim.

In the first chapter of Genesis (verse 27), man—both male and female—is created in the image of Elohim, or God. If that is the case, logic would dictate looking at Elohim first to determine just what is this image and likeness of God. But recorded history teaches us that such reasoning did not take place. Instead, people looked at humankind with all its imperfections and reasoned backwards to produce an anthropomorphic God, that is, a God made in the image and likeness of a mortal male. God became a man of war (Exodus 15:3).

According to the creation of humankind in Genesis 2 and 3, a mist clouded the lessons of the first chapter. This new God—this anthropomorphic Lord God of Genesis 2 onward—made man in the image of the Lord God's anthropomorphism. In other words, Adam loses a rib for the making of a lovely, sensual creature to tempt poor Adam beyond his ability to resist her beauty and sexual suggestions. She was made in the image and likeness of either a male rib or the serpent. Though Adam is said to be made in the image and likeness of the God of war (Exodus 15:3), he must spend his entire life alert not only about his enemies, but also alert about the temptations of a woman proven inferior because of the impurity and demonics associated with her menstruation. In all sexual encounters, Eve will forever be judged the guilty one because she was possessed: "The serpent beguiled me, and I did eat" (Genesis 3:13). The man, of course, was innocent, created by the Lord God, but tempted by his sex object, the walking, talking rib, not made in the image of God: "The woman whom thou gavest to be with me, she gave me of the tree, and I did eat" (Genesis 3:12).

According to the allegory, the woman is punished—not only to suffer the indignation associated with her menstruation—but now also burdened with multiple sorrows relating to conception and childbirth. Because she is possessed and thus incapable of making good judgments for her husband, she must be ruled by him. And the man is punished, too, because he listened to his wife.

It is easy to see why the Lord God's anthropomorphism did not include the female. She was impure, sensual, demonic. Those are the qualities of the serpent, or devil, not of God, good. In the first chapter of Genesis, the female is just as much as the image of Elohim as the male. But in the second and third, she is demoted to a creature whose sins are contagious to man. The superstitions of the early millenniums did not allow woman's being to be used to help form the inductive anthropomorphism of the Lord God, so the deductive reasoning applied to this anthropomorphism necessarily deduced only a male image and likeness. The natural conclusion then was that God is Father but not also Mother—that the image and likeness is male but not female. Even though these premises of the nature of God are not in accord with either Genesis 1 or logic, the perceived nature of God and of the image and likeness still remains only masculine for much of the Christian, Judaic, and Islamic world.

Let us put the superstitions aside for the moment and examine the nature of a non-anthropomorphic Elohim.

The name Elohim means "the strong one." It is in accord with other Scriptural sayings, such as calling Him the Almighty (Genesis 17:1) and referring to Him as omnipotent (Revelation 19:6), that is, all powerful. But if He is truly omnipotent, He must know all things, that is, be all-knowing (see I Samuel 16:7, Job 34:21, Proverbs 8:22-31, Daniel 2:20-22); and if He is truly omnipotent *or* omniscient, He has to be omnipresent, as is suggested by His names of I Am (Exodus 3:14) and I Am that I Am (Exodus 3:14)(see also Psalms 139:7-10). And His omnipotence and omniscience cannot be like Zeus', for Zeus' wife could "get away with murder" right behind his back and he would never know it unless winged Mercury or some other god or goddess told him. The reason why Zeus was not truly *all powerful*, even though he was called such, was that he did not *know* what all was happening; and he was not omniscient because he had an anthropomorphic body and thus could not be everywhere, omnipresently available when and where everything was happening. Thus an omnipotent, omniscient, omnipresent God has to be incorporeal, bodiless, or else He is more like the mythological Zeus. Incorporeality is obviously in contradistinction to the anthropomorphic bearded god painted on the ceiling of the famous Sistine Chapel.

The name *Elohim* is plural though it is usually treated as singular to conform to the Hebrew idea of one God. The singular is

*Eloah*, meaning *Deity* or *God*. In the plural, that is *Elohim*, we have not only those possible translations but according to *Strong's, the Mighty* or *Almighty* and *Goddess*. Since man, both male and female, is the image and likeness of Elohim, it should not be surprising that this name for Deity embraces both the masculine (the Almighty) and the feminine (as seen in Goddess). A plural Elohim with two natures enveloping the entire spectrum of existence, yet only one Deity.

Beginning with the second chapter of Genesis, Deity is called *Lord God*, that is, *Jehovah Elohim*. *Jehovah* means the *self-Existent* or *Eternal* but became the national name for the Jewish God. In Exodus (15:3) we read, "The Lord [Jehovah] is a man of war: the Lord is his name." Unlike in *Elohim*, there is no hint of the feminine either in the meaning of *Jehovah* or in His anthropomorphic state of "a man of war." Jehovah's truly feminine side did not evolve until after David's time.

It is apparent that Adam is made in the image and likeness of the all-male Jehovah. But what about Eve? The snake was one of the symbols for the ancient Mother Goddess, which was worshipped both before Hebrew literature and continued on as a Fertility idol found in Hebrew ruins. In the official record, the Hebrews wrote of this symbol in negative terms both to rid the culture of idolatry but also of any deific description not in accord with their all male Jehovah. The serpent in Genesis can be viewed as the Hebrew attack on the Mother Goddess; she is demonized as a lying villain that cannot be trusted. It is this serpent, not Jehovah, that Eve listens to. So whether Eve is the image and likeness of a rib or of a demon, she is not assigned a very pleasant genealogy. Her inheritance is lying and deceit, which became the degraded description of the feminine.

According to *The Interpreter's Dictionary of the Bible*, *Elohim* is a divine name and *Jehovah*, or *Yahweh*, is God's personal name.[1] Thus with God's divine name, God and the image and likeness are both masculine and feminine. However, with the personal name assigned to Him as seen through the patriarchic "glass, darkly," both God and His image and likeness are only, or almost only, masculine.

What is this image and likeness of "the invisible God" (Colossians 1:15)? According to Colossians, the invisible Christ from the foundation of the world "is the image of the invisible God, the firstborn of every creature." We are told that the Father "hath translated us into the kingdom of his dear Son" (verse 13) and that, whether Jew or gentile, the image is the "Christ in you, the hope of glory" (verse 27). Thus the image and likeness of the invisible God is not our mortality, the "creature," but "the firstborn," our spiritual self, the Christ within each one of us.

This Christian concept of an invisible God is much more like the incorporeal Elohim of Genesis 1 than the anthropomorphic Jehovah of Genesis 2. This Christian concept of the image and likeness of God, the spiritual self or Christ within us, is much more like the image and likeness of the spiritual Elohim of Genesis 1 than Jehovah's stumbling Adam, the male creature brought down by his female creature, of Genesis 2.

But what does all this have to do with the equality of women? If the image and likeness is not determined by the flesh, do women have this Christly element within *them*? If so, is it in equal portion as in men? Is the amount of Christ expressed determined by gender, or equally available to all through grace? What does expressing Christ entail? Does expressing the various qualities radiating from God the same thing as expressing Christ? Let us examine these issues for more clarity.

Biblical scholars consider the Book of Job, not as a historical story, but as religious literature designed to teach important lessons. This tradition has continued long past the Scriptures themselves and is found in many cultures, ancient and modern. Take, for example, the idea that God and His image and likeness are only masculine as plaguing men as well women. While reading the following few paragraphs reprinted here from Chapter 132 of Herman Melville's *Mody Dick*, note how everything relating to the sea is described as masculine and everything pertaining to the air, as feminine. Ask yourself as you consider in context, what does the great White Whale symbolize? What do the snow-white unspeckled birds symbolize? In context, can they symbolize the masculine and feminine natures of God?

Captain Ahab, who had lost a leg to the White Whale, has a brain like a "burnt-out crater." He does not grasp the comforting feminine blessings in the air, but stares into the masculine sea, bent on revenge on the White Whale. He is the image and likeness of the Scriptural God described as "the man of war," fighting much of the rest of the masculine and ignoring the feminine. Note at the end of the passage not only the consequences of such a focus but also the sign of hope when the feminine gently embraces Ahab's stubborn masculinity:

It was a clear steel-blue day. The firmaments of air and sea were hardly separable in that all-pervading azure; only, the pensive air was transparently pure and soft, with a woman's look, and the robust and man-like seas heaved with long, strong, lingering swells, as Samson's chest in his sleep.

Hither, and thither, on high, glided the snow-white wings of small, unspeckled birds; these were the gentle thoughts of the feminine air; but to and fro in the deeps, far down in the bottomless blue, rushed mighty Leviathans, sword-fish, and sharks; and these were the strong, troubled, murderous thinkings of the masculine sea.

But though thus contrasting within, the contrast was only in shades and shadows without; those two seemed one; it was only the sex, as it were, that distinguished them.

Aloft, like a royal czar and king, the sun seemed giving this gentle air to this bold and rolling sea; even as bride to groom. And at the girdling line of the horizon, a soft and tremulous motion—most seen here at the Equator—denoted the fond, throbbing trust, the loving alarms, with which the poor bride gave her bosom away.

Tied up and twisted; gnarled and knotted with wrinkles; haggardly firm and unyielding; his eyes glowing like coals, that still glow in the ashes of ruin; untottering Ahab stood forth in the clearness of the morn; lifting his splintered helmet of a brow to fair girl's forehead of heaven.

Oh, immortal infancy, and innocency of the azure! Invisible winged creatures that frolic all round us! Sweet childhood of air and sky! how oblivious were ye of old Ahab's close-coiled woe! But so have I seen little Miriam and Martha, laughing-eyed elves, heedlessly gambol around their old sire; sporting with the circle of singed locks which grew on the marge of that burnt-crater of his brain.

Slowly crossing the deck from the scuttle, Ahab leaned over the side and watched how his shadow in the water sank and sank to his gaze, the more and the more that he strove to pierce the profundity. But the lovely aromas in that enchanted air did at last seem to dispel, for a moment, the cankerous thing in his soul. That glad, happy air, that winsome sky, did at last stroke and caress him; the step-mother world, so long cruel—forbidding—now threw affectionate arms round his stubborn neck, and did seem to joyously sob over him, as if over one, that however willful and erring, she could yet find it in her heart to save and to bless. From beneath his slouched hat Ahab dropped a tear into the sea; nor did all the Pacific contain such wealth as that one wee drop.[2]

Ask yourself: just what was in that tear to make it wealthier than any other drop in the Pacific Ocean, even wealthier than all the other water in that ocean combined? It was not repentance because Captain Ahab continued his quest to kill the White Whale and ended up being killed in seeking his revenge. The women readers, and perhaps some of the men, may know. If men can grasp this simple point and seek more of it, both they and the world would find the human experience a lot more rewarding and pleasant.

A woman's strength does not involve sinking into Lady Macbeth's "unsex me here"[3] and then delving into Melville's "strong, troubled, murderous thinkings of the masculine sea," but instead, in touching the smallest part in the patriarchic mind of a Captain Ahab so that love will cause him to shed that tear which will add more wealth to the masculine sea than all else to be found there.

In addition, a woman can expand her strength, again not in declaring "unsex me here," but by living even more of Elohim's qualities as listed in this chapter under several synonyms for Elohim. These qualities are not limited to either gender.

Let us examine several other names for God as they have developed over the millenniums and how they have been interpreted despite superstitions, misunderstanding, prejudices, and even arrogance. When not being influenced by either patriarchy or Greek philosophy, both Augustine and Thomas Aquinas have expressed some of the most remarkably clear and deep Christian theology, especially when describing the nature of Deity. These other names are more in accord with Elohim rather than Jehovah, thus suggesting that the image and likeness *should* be regarded as both male and female.

## God as Divine Mind

The Bible tells us God has a mind (Job 23:13), and we know He must have a mind or He could not be omniscient. He must be able to have the means to think in order to be omnipotent. And His mind must be omnipresent if He is really omniscient, for He is not omniscient in the sense that Zeus was claimed to be (often in a state of ignorance). In other words, there is no place or spot where God is not; and there is no place or spot where His mind is not. Therefore, God is His Mind; or God is Mind, the "one omnipresent Mind" of the universe.

Over the centuries of the Christian era, a number of both Catholic and Protestant theologians and literacy scholars have addressed Deity as Mind. These writers have demonstrated that the concept of Elohim as divine Mind has remained constant over the centuries, yet usually the image and likeness of Elohim, or Mind, which is recorded in the first chapter of Genesis as being both male and female, is rejected for Jehovah's image's being all male, a rejection that excludes women.

Let us view a few statements illustrating God as Mind and then, at the end of this section, examine what this name *should* indicate about women in the spirit of Elohim. The exemplary list of quotes that follows here is not intended to be exhaustive. We will begin with Europe and the western part of the Middle East.

St. Gregory (331?-394?), Bishop of Nyssa, in his *On the Making of Man*, referred to God as "the very Mind."[4]

Thrice, in his *The City of God*, St. Augustine (354-430) referred to God as "the divine mind."[5]

St. John of Damascus (676-770), Governor of Damascus, wrote in his *Exposition of the Orthodox Faith*: "God then is called Mind and Reason and Spirit and Wisdom and Power, as the cause of these, and as immaterial, and maker of all, and omnipotent."[6]

Seven times, within a short space in his *Summa Theologica*, St. Thomas Aquinas (1225-1274) called God either "mind" or "the divine mind."[7]

Dante Alighieri (1265-1321) in his *The Inferno*, as translated by the American poet and scholar John Ciardi, called God "the Eternal

Mind."[8] Although *Mind* here is used to rhyme with *combined* in the translation of poetry into English poetry, Ciardi apparently was capturing Dante's understanding of Deity as evidenced in a prose translation of Dante's *Paradise* done decades earlier by Charles Eliot Norton, where Dante called God both "the Divine Mind" and "the sole Intelligence."[9]

René Descartes (1596-1650), who was schooled by the Jesuits and always found residence near a university and a Catholic church, in his *Objections against the Meditations and Replies*, referred to "the Divine intellect."[10]

Benedict de Spinoza (1632-1677), though born Jewish, was cut off by the Jewish authorities for his unorthodox views. So he associated with various Christian groups. In his *Ethics* he reasoned that "God's intellect, will, and power are one and the same thing" and that "the intellect of God...constitute[d] His essence"[11] and called Deity "an infinite thinking Being."[12]

Leaving the continent and crossing the channel to Britain, we start with John Locke (1632-1704). Within three pages, in his *Concerning Human Understanding*, he called God "eternal Mind" thrice, "eternal infinite Mind," "thinking eternal Being," "eternal thinking Being," and "eternal, immaterial, thinking Being."[13]

Next we find Samuel T. Coleridge (1772-1834) and William Wordsworth (1770-1850), both poetic colleagues expounding God as Mind. In his poem "Religious Musings," Coleridge referred to "the infinite mind" (line 408) and wrote, "There is one Mind, one omnipresent Mind,/Omnific" (lines 105-106). Wordsworth, in his "Ode: Intimations of Immortality from Recollections of Early Childhood," penned the deific phrase "the Eternal Mind" (line 113). (Some anthologies capitalize the *E* and *M* here and others do not.)

James Hastings (1860-1922), Scottish divine and scholar, in the first paragraph of his discussion of *time* in his *Dictionary of the Bible*, called God "the Divine mind."[14]

Crossing the pond to America, we see the tradition continued. A quick check of almost any modern dictionary printed in the United States reveals that Christian Scientists use *Mind* as a synonym for *God*. Their Leader, Mary Baker Eddy (1821-1910), used this term and others with and without various adjectives throughout her several books.[15]

In his play *Our Town*, Thornton Wilder (1897-1975) introduced Mind in an interesting format. At the end of act one, Rebecca tells of an address on an envelope "Jane Crofut; The Crofut Farm;

Grover's Corners; Sutton County; New Hampshire; United States of America." After an interruption by her brother, which sets off the rest, she continues: "The United States of America; Continent of North America; Western Hemisphere; the Earth; the Solar System; the Universe; the Mind of God."[16] Perhaps Wilder could have inserted the Milky Way Galaxy between "the Solar System" and "the Universe," but that is neither here nor there, as the expression goes. The point is that the playwright saw everything in the Universe as being in the Mind of God, thus emphasizing Mind's omnipresence.

In Paramount Pictures' 1956 movie *The Ten Commandments*, when Moses had returned from the mount of the burning bush, he slowly approached his wife and Joshua. As Joshua questioned him, Moses said, "He revealed His Word to my mind. The Word was God." Joshua asked, "Did He speak as a man?" Moses responded, "He is not flesh, but Spirit, the Light of eternal Mind, and I know that His Light is in every man."

In 1974, Paul Lee Tan, Th.D., wrote in his book *The Interpretation of Prophecy*,

> *On infinite mind and the written words.*—Concerning the reasoning that Infinite Mind should not be confined to mere words and thus a double sense should be sought, we state that God is not trying to reveal in Scripture all that He knows—only what He intends man to know. The prophet Moses is clear: "The secret things belong unto the Lord our God; but those things which are revealed belong unto us and to our children forever" (Deut. 29:29).[17]

Not only theologians and literary people have thought of God as Mind. Today some scientists are considering the idea. For example, quantum physics professor Fred Alan Wolf, UCLA, as have other quantum physicists, has been analyzing the meaning of numerous studies which indicate that the results change when an observer is introduced. Thought or consciousness affects light, sound, and water, for instance. He concludes that "there is a creative power in the universe." He rejects the notion that God is some kind of humanoid being, a monarch sitting on some throne up there, "whipping us into shape." And likewise he rejects the opposite notion that there is no creative power, only the sparks of electricity operating without purpose. Based upon what he has found in quantum physics, he concludes that "there is an intelligent presence; there is a one-mindedness: that I call it, or God, if you want to call it that."[18]

Physics professor Paul Davies of Arizona State University writes of his book *The Mind of God*:

> The title is taken from the closing passage in Stephen Hawking's famous book [*A Brief History of Time*]. This is my attempt to really get to grips with the science and religion debate. I focus on the idea of God as the rational ground that supports the law-like order in the universe. I see science as a way of uncovering the deep and elegant mathematical structure in nature – of 'glimpsing the mind of God,' as Hawking expressed it. But where did this mathematical order come from? And could it have been different? Why is the universe so astonishingly bio-friendly? Does it just *look* contrived or is it *in fact* contrived?[19]

Professor Davies concludes in his book, "I cannot believe that our existence in this universe is a mere quirk of fate, an accident of history, an incidental blip in the great cosmic drama. ... Through conscious beings the universe has generated self-awareness. This can be no trivial detail, no minor byproduct of mindless, purposeless forces. We are truly meant to be here."[20]

The last three paragraphs deal with scientists from quantum physics to astrophysics. But what about biology's equivalent to quantum physics: molecular biology. These biologists have found that a single cell has thousands of proteins with interlocking shapes linked in a chain. There are about 20 amino acids and 30,000 distinct proteins with about 100-300 amino acids combining in different combinations to make just one of these 30,000. Furthermore, the sequence of constructing these combinations is as important as which amino acids are chosen. Consequently, some molecular biologists see such an irreducible complexity just to form one protein of the thousands in a single cell that these scientists are questioning how such a process could be due to chance. One mathematician, Dr. William Dumbski of Baylor University, has concluded that the formation of one protein due to chance would be about 1 in the number 1 followed by 100 zeroes. This is "way beyond anything we can reasonably attribute to chance."[21]

Just think a moment: the human body has about 100 trillion cells and each of these cells has thousands of proteins formed as described above. How did we get here if *not* one protein can be formed by chance?

Medical studies have their results judged significant, that is, beyond chance, if the margin of error due to chance is equal to or less than 1 divided by the number of 1 followed by just *two* zeroes (100), and near absolute perfection of the 1 followed by just *three* zeroes (1,000). How can Darwinists argue with such significance in cell research when the margin of error is equal to or less than 1 divided by the number 1 followed by a *hundred* zeroes!?! Because some minds can be stuck on preconceived 150-year-old notions that modern microscopes have proven wrong. Thought stuck on such notions just cannot accept the facts.

In 1859, Charles Darwin published his *On the Origin of Species*. He argued that all life was the result of undirected natural processes: time, chance, and natural selection. The microscopes of his day could let him see a cell but not its insides. Today, with microscopes that magnify things 50,000 times, molecular biologists can study the inside of cells and all their complex parts. Darwin, as smart as he was, if he could have seen inside those cells, probably would be in agreement with these biologists today who conclude that natural selection may explain the *survival* of the fittest but it cannot explain the *arrival* of the fittest.[22]

These questions of chance and natural selection in the beginning of biological life brought a group of scientists, mathematicians, and other thinkers together at Pajaro Dunes, California, in 1993. They came from as far away as Cambridge, Munich, and the University of Chicago. At least two situations they discussed stand out. First, even if amino acids could have formed by chance on an earth surface that was not conducive to doing such, they could not have sequenced themselves by chance to form all the protein into a cell: the DNA for the protein of a cell would fill hundreds of pages in a book. And to replicate, DNA has a little engineering motor that opens the DNA strand so that other motors can run the duplication process. Where did these little motors come from? If they are needed for DNA to replicate and DNA is needed for proteins to replicate, then, even before a living cell could be produced, did not there have to be some information available from DNA? Information implies intelligence, some intelligence available before biological life. And don't information and intelligence call into question some aspects of chance and natural selection?[23]

The other situation that stands out from the discussion at Pajaro Dunes in 1993 has to deal with the irreducible complexity of the bacterial flagellum of e-coli. It runs like the gears in a motor, a structure with 30 of its 40 parts unique—drive shaft, propeller, like an outboard motor of a boat. In moving the tail, it runs at 100 rpm, can stop within a quarter of a rotation, and immediately go 100 rpm in a different direction. One biologist referred to this motor as the most efficient machine on the planet. But if any one part were missing, it would not work. All the parts have to be there at the same time, or natural selection would slowly eliminate them one by one.[24]

Equally interesting is the sequencing of construction of this motor. Each part must be assembled in a specific order from the inside out. It is like building a house: first you put in the foundation. Then comes the outer wall frame. Then the roof, the outer wall shell, the windows, the wiring and plumbing, the installation, inner wall shells, painting and other details. Can you imagine a house falling together all by chance, without *any* intelligent design or purpose? This is the question these scientists were asking themselves about the bacterial flagellum motor.[25]

In 1996, Dr. Michael J. Behe, biochemist at LeHigh University, published a book, *Darwin's Black Box*, in which in chapter 9 he attributed the formation of the bacterial flagellum to what he called *intelligent design*. As one can imagine, this idea created a storm of controversy. Christians immediately adopted the term. Darwinists accused Dr. Behe and other such scientists of introducing religion into the science laboratory. In reply, Dr. Behe and Dr. Scott Minnich of the University of Idaho, among others, pointed out that although the term *intelligent design* may have some religious implications, it has *no* religious premises. It is based solely on a combination of observation not available to Darwin, of mathematics, and of logic.[26]

I have not seen or heard of any discussion or article that covers the next question I propose, although someone else may have raised it. Can the *intelligence* in the intelligent design of a cell be the same, or related to, the *consciousness* that quantum physicists have found altering light, sound, and water? The quantum physicist Fred Alan Wolfe quoted earlier referred to this consciousness as "one mindedness," but granted some may prefer the term God.

As we have seen, some theologians, literary writers, and

scientists have concluded—from various positions, of course—that some kind of supreme intelligence exists, even before biological life. Some call it Mind.

So if God is divine Mind, is Deity masculine, feminine, or both? Today, those in the West who need not subjugate women to psychologically justify their own self-worth recognize that women can think as well as men and sometimes better. But when the inaccurate and false syllogisms were being formulated about woman's thinking ability, the views were quite different. Men were logical beings, and women, only emotional ones. Thus for the most part men with means were educated while women were steered toward a domestic life with a focus on the duties of a wife and mother. Not being educated, women were held ignorant in the academic spheres. But *ignorance* means lack of knowledge while *lack of intelligence* means lack in the ability to think. I was continually amazed as an English professor to find the number of college students who equated the two. Just because I am ignorant on how to bake a cake from scratch doesn't mean that I cannot think. As long as I have some decent level of intelligence, I can always open a cookbook and educate myself. But when the old syllogisms were being formed, women were considered nothing but emotional, ignorant creatures who lacked the ability to think clearly. Consequently, the divine Mind, it was reasoned, must be masculine and He made these feminine creatures inferior to men, the true image and likeness. The cyclic reasoning is pathetic! The syllogistic conclusion of inferiority still hangs on even though the premises have been shown to be false.

Allan G. Johnson contends that many of the great qualities of humanity should not be relegated to manhood but to adulthood. He points out that these qualities are ever much as feminine as they are masculine, that the two sexually oriented genders are much more similar by nature than different, and that examination of actuality shows they, contrary to our patriarchally cultural society's convention, certainly are not "two opposite sorts of human beings."[27]

One English translation of Genesis 1:26, 27 from an Icelandic Bible that had been translated from Martin Luther's German Bible reads as follows:

> God said, Be it our wish to process man after our
> mind, after our likeness. ... And God created man

after His mind; after God's mind created He him; He
created them male and female.

The equating of God and His mind in Genesis 1 is significant
because the original term in Hebrew is the non-anthropomorphic
Elohim. In essence, both male *and* female are shaped in the image
of the divine Mind.

Is it conceivable then that women, as well as men, can express
similar qualities that are the hues of Mind? That they both, for
example, can be alert, aware, capable, Christ-minded (Philippians
2:5), clear, coherent, comprehensive, courageous, creative, decisive,
discerning, discretional, disposed to concentrating, eloquent,
enlightening, enduring, focused, innovative, insightful, intelligent,
intuitive, inventive, harmonious with others, knowledgeable, mentally
strong, motivated, observant, original, patient, prone to listening,
prudent, perceptive, receptive, resilient, resourceful, righteously
judging, spiritually minded (Romans 8:6), understanding, unique,
wise, and so on throughout infinity? Cannot both sexes labor in
the harvest fields of divine Mind, reaping the qualities of Mind?[28]

## God as Eternal Life

In the Bible we read that "he [the Lord thy God] is thy life..."
(Deuteronomy 30:20). King David reportedly penned in a psalm to
God, "For with thee is the fountain of life" (Psalms 36:9). In the first,
God is apparently declared to be Life. In the second and similar
passages, it is implied that He is Life. Following are a few examples
that adopt this theme.

In his *Third Ennead*, Plotinus (205-270) wrote:

A close enough definition of Eternity would be that
it is a life limitless in the full sense of being all the
life there is and a life which, knowing nothing of
past or future to shatter its completeness, possesses
itself intact for ever. To the notion of a Life (a Living-
Principle) all-comprehensive add that it never
spends itself, and we have the statement of Life
instantaneously infinite."[29]

St. Augustine in his *Confessions* addressed God, "Thou Thyself art supremely Essence and Life"[30] and "So also did I endeavour to conceive of Thee, Life of my life, as vast, through infinite spaces, on every side penetrating the whole mass of the universe, and beyond it, every way, through unmeasurable boundless spaces...."[31]

Likewise, Thomas Aquinas in his *Summa Theologica* drew the following conclusions: "In Him principally is life."[32] "As God is His own very being and understanding, so is He His own life...."[33] "Whatever is in God as understood is the very living or life of God. ... It follows that all things in Him are the divine life itself,"[34] and "Hence the ideas of things, though not living in themselves, are life in the divine mind, as having a divine being in that mind."[35]

Dozens of writers refer to God as Being, First Being, Eternal Being, Supreme Being, Absolute Universal Being, or I AM. *Being* relates to actual reality or life. The implication is that the Eternal Being is Life. Also, dozens of authors refer to God as Divine Essence or Essence with some other superlative adjective. *Essence* comes from the Latin root *esse, to be.* Thus these references also imply a God of divine Life. When *creator* is added to Being, substance, absolute Essence, the implication is reinforced that God is Life. There are so many such references that I have not attempted to list them.

It was not until about 1827 that human females were found to have eggs. Aristotle, like the other Greek philosophers whose ideas still penetrate thought in many cultures, had drawn conclusions about mankind based upon what he supposedly observed in animals. Apparently, he never opened a chicken egg and noticed the male's contribution attached to the female's yoke. In humans, semen one could see, but eggs were too small to be seen without a microscope, which did not exist in those days. If one could see it, it existed; if one could not see it, it did not exist. Thus only men were thought to be the source of human life. The woman was thought to control the sex of the fetus according to her water containment, whatever that meant.

Let's look at an example, using Henry VIII of England. Henry wanted a male heir but was unaware that his semen controlled the sex of his potential children. If a wife produced only a daughter (except for a son who died at childbirth), what was Henry's solution? Get another woman with better water containment.

Ages ago women were honored as the source of life. But with the coming of patriarchy, men were thought to be the only contributors to the fetus' life and thus Life itself must also be only masculine. And the image and likeness of this male Life must be men only, not women. There's that pathetic, cyclic reasoning again! Thus, ignorance not only shaped the anthropomorphic Lord God, that man of war (Exodus 15:3); it has also tainted the perception of the non-anthropomorphic divine Life. Consequently, even though the image and likeness of the non-anthropomorphic Elohim embraced both male and female, its revised, tainted definition influenced by the anthropomorphic version of Lord God left the female out of the image and likeness. Thus women, it was concluded, were inferior beings, if beings at all.

Since woman was thought to contribute nothing to the formation of human life (except for its sex and the ancients even got that wrong), only to serve as an incubator, in the sixteenth century Paracelsus suggested in his book *De Generatione Rerum* that the worthless woman be done away with altogether in the baby's formation by incubating human semen in horse manure.[36]

Apparently, Biology 101 was different back in those days.

Since the formation of human life is dependent upon contributions from women as well as men, is it conceivable that God, infinite Life, is feminine as well as masculine? If so, is not God Mother as well as Father? Not just Father, as our patriarchic culture has insisted on, nor just Mother, as some twentieth-century feminist writers have asserted, but both, both Father-Mother, one God with an image and likeness that includes both males and females?

As stated before, Allan G. Johnson claims that humanity's great qualities—both masculine and feminine—are not limited to manhood but found throughout adulthood.[37] Is it conceivable then that women, as well as men, can express similar qualities that are the hues of Life? That they both can be active, boundlessly blissful, bountiful, energetic, enterprising, expressing harmony and goodness, feeling whole, free, healthy, lively, mobile, persistent, tenacious, vivacious, zealous? "When we have shuffled off this mortal coil," as Shakespeare's Hamlet put it, (and even before then to some degree according to some Christians), can the male and female live on expressing agelessness, eternal existence, immortality, inorganic being, permanence, perpetuity, timelessness, and so on throughout infinity? Cannot both sexes labor in the harvest fields of eternal Life, reaping the qualities of Life?

# God as infinite Spirit

Besides the names *God* and *Lord God*, perhaps *Spirit* is the next most frequently mentioned name for God in the Scriptures. It appears about forty times in the Old Testament, often as *Spirit of God* or *Spirit of the Lord*, with *Spirit* either capitalized or not, depending on the translator, and about twice that many times in the New Testament, often as just *Spirit* when not referring to the holy spirit, that is, the holy ghost. The Master himself was reported to have said, "God is a Spirit: and they that worship him must worship him in spirit and in truth" (John 4:24).

The Scriptures also offer some correlation between Spirit and the previous two names for God already covered. For example, a correlation between God as divine Mind and God as Spirit in the expression "the mind of the Spirit" (Romans 8:27) and between God as eternal Life and God as infinite Spirit in the expression "the Spirit of life from God" (Revelation 11:11). As a side note, the Greek word νευμα (*pneuma*), which is translated *Spirit* in the passage from John in the previous paragraph ("God is a Spirit"), can also be translated as *Mind* or *the Life-Principle*.

Along these same lines, one might note a definition of *Spirit* in *The Compact Edition* of *The Oxford English Dictionary*: After defining *Spirit* as an

> incorporeal or immaterial being, as opposed to *body* or *matter*; being or intelligence conceived as distinct from, or independent of, anything physical or material, the dictionary suggests in parentheses that the reader compare this definition with one listed under *Mind*.[38]

The idea that God is Spirit is found in both the Old and New Testaments, as cited above. Let's now examine some of the many references to God as Spirit by other writers. There was a flurry of such references in the fourth century of the Christian era. St. Bazil (329?-379), Archbishop of Caesarea, had several things to say on the subject. Perhaps the beginning of Chapter IX of his book *On the Spirit* is most representative:

> Let us now investigate what are our common conceptions concerning the Spirit, as well those

which have been gathered by us from Holy Scripture concerning It as those which we have received from the unwritten traditions of the Fathers. First of all we ask, who on hearing the titles of the Spirit is not lifted up in soul, who does not raise his conception to the supreme nature? It is called "Spirit of God," "Spirit of truth which proceedeth from the Father," "right Spirit," "a leading Spirit." Its proper and peculiar title is "Holy Spirit;" which is a name specially appropriate to everything that is incorporeal, purely immaterial, and indivisible. So our Lord, when teaching the woman who thought God to be an object of local worship that the incorporeal is incomprehensible, said "God is a spirit." On our hearing, then, of a spirit, it is impossible to form the idea of a nature circumscribed, subject to change and variation, or at all like the creature. We are compelled to advance in our conceptions to the highest, and to think of an intelligent essence, in power infinite, in magnitude unlimited, unmeasured by times or ages, ... perfecting all other things, but Itself in nothing lacking; living not as needing restoration, but as Supplier of life; not growing by additions, but straightway full, self-established, omnipresent, ... filling all things with Its power. ...[39]

St. Gregory Nazinanzen (331?-391), Archbishop of Constantinople, wrote in his "On the Holy Spirit" as *The Fifth Theological Oration* that

for the present it will suffice to say that it is the Spirit in Whom we worship, and in Whom we pray. For Scripture says, God is a Spirit, and they that worship Him must worship Him in Spirit and in truth. And again,—we know not what we should pray for as we ought; but the Spirit Itself maketh intercession for us with groanings which cannot be uttered; and I will pray with the Spirit and I will pray with the understanding also;—that is, in the mind and in the Spirit.[40]

St. Ambrose (340-397), Bishop of Milan, wrote in his *Of the Holy Spirit,*

> The Holy Spirit ... is uncircumscribed and infinite, Who infused Himself into the minds of the disciples throughout the separate divisions of distant regions, and the remote bounds of the whole world, Whom nothing is able to escape or to deceive. And therefore holy David says: "Whither shall I go from Thy Spirit, or whither shall I flee from Thy face."[41]

In the same book, he penned:

> And as it is said the Word of Life, so, too, the Spirit of Life. Therefore, as the Word of Life is Life, so, too, the Spirit of Life is Life.[42]

St. Jerome (340?-420), Latin scholar, wrote in his Letter LVIII:

> I do not presume to limit God's omnipotence or to restrict to a narrow strip of earth Him whom the heaven cannot contain. Each believer is judged not by his residence in this place or in that but according to the deserts of his faith. The true worshippers worship the Father neither at Jerusalem nor on mount Gerizim: for "God is a spirit, and they that worship Him must worship Him in spirit and in truth" ...[43]

Three centuries later, John of Damascus (about 676-770), Governor of Damascus and Greek theologian, declared in his *Exposition of the Orthodox Faith*: "God ... is called Mind and Reason and Spirit and Wisdom and Power, as the cause of these, and as immaterial, and maker of all, and omnipotent."[44]

Moving on to the nineteenth century, Richard Trench, in his famous *The Parables of Our Lord*, used the expression in his chapter on the ten virgins, "the informing Spirit of God which prompts the works and quickens the faith."[45]

Poets, too, have addressed God as Spirit. For example, William Wordsworth in "The Prelude" (line 401) called out, "Wisdom and Spirit of the universe!" Samuel T. Coleridge in "This Lime-tree Bower My Prison" (line 42) referred to God as "the Almighty Spirit." And Lord Byron in the first line of his "Sonnet on Chillon" addressed God as "Eternal Spirit of the chainless Mind!"

In the twenty-first century, most Christian denominations accept the words of the Master: "God is a Spirit: and they that worship him must worship him in spirit and in truth" (John 4:24). The tradition is well established.

Today, with plenty of exceptions of course with both genders, generally women are considered more spiritually minded and pure than men. But back when the syllogisms of women's inferiority were being formed, women were thought to be materially minded and impure because of their menstruation—a monthly punishment for their sins. Men were spiritually-minded, pure, courageous—the hues of Spirit found in Spirit's image and likeness. Women were unfit for sacred office. They needed to stay home and repent while doing domestic chores. (For one thing, working at home should not be considered a bad thing—not as punishment, not as a sign of inferiority, not as less-valued work.)

For another thing, as mentioned before, Wisdom in the Old Testament was discussed as feminine, even as a feminine personification. And Wisdom (sometimes also called by the name Sophia, derived from the Greek word for Wisdom) was associated with Spirit, often also considered to be feminine.[46] Thus Spirit, based upon both ancient and modern usage, has to be both feminine and masculine.

Therefore, both men and women can similarly express the vast qualities of Spirit: boldness, boundless bliss, cleanliness, conscientiousness, consistency, courage, diligence, dominion, eagerness, effervescence, efficiency, effortlessness, empathy, endurance, energy, enthusiasm, exhilaration, exuberance, fearlessness, freedom, goodness, grace, gusto, holiness, illumination, innocence, incorporeality (being absent from the body and present with the Lord, as Paul taught), independence, inspiration, intuition, joy, liberty, light, mightiness, morality, naturalness, omnipresence (again, being absent from the body and present with the Lord), omnipotence (being able to do any will God has for us), oneness (atonement, or at-one-ment), openness, peace, permanency, perseverance, positiveness, power (of God), presence, purity, radiance, renewal, resolve, resourcefulness, serenity, sinlessness, solidarity, spirituality, spontaneity, steadfastness, strength, sweetness, thoroughness, tranquility, unfoldment, unity, willingness, zest, and so on through infinity. Cannot both men and women labor in the harvest fields of infinite Spirit, reaping the qualities of Spirit?

# God as Absolute Truth

In John 18:37, 38, we read of a conversation between Jesus and Pilate: "To this end was I born, and for this cause came I into the world, that I should bear witness unto the truth. Every one that is of the truth heareth my voice. Pilate saith unto him, What is truth?"

That question did not receive a response. Jesus had already answered it in both his words and his works. For example, Jesus had told the woman in Samaria, "God is a Spirit: and they that worship him must worship him in spirit and in truth" (John 4:24). If Spirit is God as expressed in "in spirit," then can "in truth" be saying that Truth is also God? Furthermore, Pilate, not that familiar with Jewish literature, was not aware that the Jews' King David had addressed their God in a Psalm as "O Lord God of truth" (31: 5). Later, one of Jesus' disciples would write in his first epistle: "And it is the Spirit that beareth witness, because the Spirit is truth" (I John 5:6).

The concept that God is Truth is more closely related to the incorporeal Elohim than to an anthropomorphic Being. Let's examine what some writers have said on the subject.

Two of the early Christian writers place Truth in the Godhead. Athanasius (298?-373), Bishop of Alexandria, referred to the divine as Truth in his *Defence Before Constantius*.[47] St. Basil the Great (329?-379), Archbishop of Caesarea, wrote that "He is Himself truth. ..."[48]

St. Augustine (354-430) wrote of God being Truth numerous times, most of which are found in his *Confessions*. Here are a few examples:

> They cried out "Truth, Truth," and spake much thereof to me, "yet it was not in them" [see I John 2:4]: but they spake falsehood, not of Thee only (who truly art Truth), but even of those elements of this world, Thy creatures. And I indeed ought to have passed by even philosophers who spake truth concerning them, for love of Thee, my Father, supremely good, Beauty of all things beautiful. O Truth, Truth, how inwardly did even then the marrow of my soul pant after thee.... I hungered and thirsted not even after those first works of Thine, but after Thee Thyself,

the Truth, "in whom is no variableness, neither shadow of turning" [James 1:17]....[49]

They discourse many things truly concerning the creature; but Truth, Artificer [artistic worker] of the creature, they seek not piously, and therefore find Him not; or if they find Him, knowing Him to be God, they glorify Him not as God, neither are thankful [Romans 1:21], but become vain in their imaginations, and profess themselves to be wise [Romans 1:22], attributing to themselves what is Thine; and thereby with most perverse blindness, study to impute to Thee what is their own, forging lies of Thee Who are the Truth, and changing the glory of the uncorruptible God into an image made like corruptible man, and to birds, and four-footed beasts, and creeping things [Romans 1:23], changing Thy truth into a lie, and worshipping and serving the creature more than the Creator [Romans 1:25].[50]

He that knows the Truth knows what that Light is; and he that knows It knows eternity. Love knoweth it. O Truth Who art Eternity! And Love Who art Truth! And Eternity Who art Love! Thou art my God, to Thee do I sigh night and day.[51]

I saw that they owed their being to Thee, and were all bounded in Thee, but in a different way: not as being in space, but because Thou containest all things in Thine hand in Thy Truth; and all things are true so far as they be; nor is there any falsehood, unless when that is thought to be which is not. And I saw that all things did harmonize, not with their places only, but with their seasons.[52]

Seeing I did so judge, I had found the unchangeable and true Eternity of Truth, above my changeable mind.[53]

Whereas then I cannot enquire of him [Moses], Thee, Thee I beseech, O Truth, full of Whom he [Moses] spake truth, Thee, my God, I beseech, forgive my sins; and Thou, who gavest him Thy servant to speak these things, give to me also to understand them.[54]

Eight hundred years later, Thomas Aquinas (1225-1274) in his *Summa Theologica* referred to God as truth and the First Truth:

> The existence of truth is self-evident. For whoever denies the existence of truth grants that truth does not exist. And, if truth does not exist, then the proposition "Truth does not exist" is true. And if there is anything true, there must be truth. But God is truth itself. ... The existence of truth in general is self-evident, but the existence of a First Truth is not self-evident to us.[55]
>
> His being is not only conformed to His intellect, but it is the very act of His intellect, and His act of understanding is the measure and cause of every other being and of every other intellect, and He Himself is His own being and act of understanding. And so it follows not only that truth is in Him, but that he is truth itself, and the supreme and first truth. ... If we speak of divine truth in its essence, we cannot understand this unless the affirmative must be resolved into the negative, as when one says: "the Father is of Himself, because He is not from another." Similarly, the divine truth can be called "a likeness to the principle," inasmuch as His being is not different from His intellect.[56]

Dante Alighieri, usually referred to just as Dante (1265-1321), was just a child when Thomas Aquinas died. In his *Paradise* portion of *The Divine Comedy*, Dante referred to Aquinas' *Summa Theologica* and then in the same paragraph used Aquinas' term "the first truth": "There will be seen that which we hold by faith, not demonstrated, but it will be known of itself like the first truth which man believes."[57]

Georg Wilhelm Friedrick Hegel (1770-1831), a German philosopher, in his *Philosophy of History* used the phrase "assurance of the eternal, of absolute truth, the truth of God."[58]

William Wordsworth (1770-1850), British poet, thrice in his "The Prelude; or, Growth of a Poet's Mind," made reference to a highest truth. Two are worth examining:

Then doubt is not, and truth is more than truth, —
A hope it is, and a desire; a creed
Of zeal, by an authority Divine.
                    (Book Ninth, lines 404-406)
With zeal expanding in Truth's holy light.
                    (Book Tenth, line 138)

In the first quote from St. Augustine in this section on Truth, Augustine, you may recall, equated the Father both with Beauty and with Truth. While reading that, I could not help recalling the last two lines of "Ode on a Grecian Urn" by John Keats (1795-1821):

'Beauty is truth, truth beauty,'—that is all
Ye know on earth, and all ye need to know.

So how does all this relate to women?

Thomas Aquinas, for the most part, was brilliant in expressing theology, but his views of women were contaminated by ancient Greek mythology, especially, Aristotle's works. He began his theological studies in Paris in 1245 under the master Albert the Great (1206-1280). The complete works of Aristotle had been lost until recently then discovered in Arabic. Albert became the champion of Aristotle, and Thomas, his most able student, followed suit, taking the Greek philosopher's ideas, including those about women, and Christianizing them. Corrupted Christianity moved from Christ's idea of women (and Plato's, as adopted by St. Augustine 800 years before Aquinas) to Aristotle's diabolical views of females. The following is what Albert wrote about women and taught his most famous student (I have added comments in brackets):

The woman contains more liquid than the man, and it is a property of liquid to take things up easily and to hold onto them poorly. [This is ancient Greek mythology.] Liquids are easily moved, hence women are inconstant and curious. [This is clearly Aristotle.] ... Woman is a misbegotten man and has a faulty and defective nature in comparison with his. [Aristotle again.] Therefore she is unsure in herself. What she herself cannot get she seeks to obtain through lying and diabolical deceptions. [Aristotle through and through] And so, to put it briefly, one must be on guard with every woman, as if she were a poisonous snake and the horned devil. [She is the descendant of Eve, made in the image and likeness of the deceitful serpent in Genesis 2 and bloated into the horned monster of Revelation.][59]

Such a description can be nothing further from the truth. Yes, some women may be deceitful, but deceitfulness is not limited by gender. Under Aristotelian Christianity, whatever happened to the image and likeness of Elohim in Genesis 1?

Since Aristotle's views still permeate much of Christianity, many men are drunk from drinking the blood of this ancient Greek philosopher. Others who have stopped sipping the cup of Aristotle are confused from their hangover. A few have found the cup and the bread from Truth's table.

The fact is that Truth unveils Its image and likeness to anyone who manifests the qualities of Truth. With myths and superstitions set aside, the truth is that anyone living in the great heart of Truth is living the image and likeness of Truth and receives Truth's birthright.

The great heart of Elohim is open to all, both male and female. Therefore, both men and women can similarly express the vast qualities of Truth: accuracy, actuality, authenticity, beauty, candor, certainty, Christliness, clearness, correctness, decency, dependability, directness, exactness, faultlessness, fidelity, flawlessness, frankness, freedom, good judgment, honesty, genuineness, honor, hopefulness, intactness, integrity, justice, liberty, loyalty, magnificence, obedience, perfection (in accord with the divine Mind and not the mortal), precision, permanence, reality, regeneration, righteousness, rightness (with humility), sincerity, straightforwardness, triumph, trustworthiness, understanding, uprightness, validity, veracity, verity, victory, virtue, wholeness, and so on throughout infinity. Cannot both men and women labor in the harvest fields of Truth, reaping the qualities of Truth?

## God as Divine Love

Perhaps the most beloved name of God, at least in Christianity, is that of *Love*. Although many passages in the Bible bring out God's love, perhaps the ones most quoted are found in John's first epistle, chapter 4:

> 7 Beloved, let us love one another: for love is of God; and every one that loveth is born of God, and knoweth God.

> 8 He that loveth not knoweth not God; for God is love.

> 11 Beloved, if God so loved us, we ought also to love one another.

> 12 No man hath seen God at any time. If we love one another, God dwelleth in us, and his love is perfected in us.

> 13 Hereby know we that we dwell in him, and he in us, because he hath given us of his Spirit.

> 16 And we have known and believed the love that God hath to us. God is love; and he that dwelleth in love dwelleth in God, and God in him.

The idea that God is Love is found in much of Christian literature, and the words adorn a wall in many churches and chapels. The following are a few examples found in the literature.

Gregory of Nyssa (331?-394?), a Greek father of the church, after identifying God as Mind in his *On the Making of Man*, wrote, "Again, God is love, and the fount of love: for this the great John declares, that 'love is of God,' and 'God is love.'"[60] In his *On the Soul and the Resurrection*, he penned:

> The life of the Supreme Being is love, seeing that the Beautiful is necessarily lovable to those who recognize it, and the Deity does recognize it, and so this recognition becomes love, that which He recognizes being essentially beautiful. This True Beauty the insolence of satiety cannot touch; and no satiety interrupting this continuous capacity to love the Beautiful, God's life will have its activity

in love; which life is thus in itself beautiful, and is essentially of a loving disposition towards the Beautiful, and receives no check to this activity of love.[61]

John Cassian (4th-5th century), a reclusive religious writer, included in his *Conferences* one titled *First Conference of Abbot Joseph*. The title of Chapter XIII reads, "How love does not only belong to God but is God." The first two sentences of this short chapter states,

> Finally so highly is the virtue of love extolled that the blessed Apostle John declares that it not only belongs to God but that it is God saying: "God is love; he therefore that abideth in love, abideth in God, and God in him." For so far do we see that it is divine, that we find that what the Apostle says is plainly a living truth in us: "For the love of God is shed abroad in our hearts by the Holy Ghost Who dwelleth in us" [Romans 5:5].[62]

The following passage from St. Augustine was also cited in the section considering God as Truth:

> He that knows the Truth knows what that Light is; and he that knows It knows eternity. Love knoweth it. O Truth Who art Eternity! And Love Who art Truth! And Eternity Who art Love! Thou art my God, to Thee do I sigh night and day.[63]

In his *Summa Theologica*, Thomas Aquinas quoted I John 4:16 where John wrote "God is love,"[64] identified Love as a name for God,[65] and wrote that "the Holy Spirit is Love."[66]

Dante referred to God as Love three times in his *The Divine Comedy*. In *The Inferno*, he addressed God as "Love Divine."[67] In his *Purgatory*, he called God "Eternal Love."[68] And in his *Paradise*, Dante, paralleling his "the first truth," a phrase he had taken from Aquinas for God, referred to God also as "the First Love."[69]

Leo Tolstoy (1828-1910), in his famous Russian epic *War and Peace*, related the thoughts of Prince Andrew as he was dying:

"Love? What is love?" he thought.
"Love hinders death. Love is life. All, everything
that I understand, I understand only because I love.
Everything is, everything exists, only because I love.
Everything is united by it alone. Love is God, and to
die means that I, a particle of love, shall return to
the general and eternal source."[70]

Samuel T. Coleridge (1772-1834), British romantic poet, perhaps
summarized God as completely and yet succinctly as any in his
poem "Religious Musings":

There is one Mind, one omnipresent Mind,
Omnific. His most holy name is Love. (lines 105, 106)

Today the biblical words "God is Love" are carved into or painted
on the walls of many Christian churches and Sunday schools.
Men in the past have tried to usurp "God is Love" as being totally
masculine, but there can be no denying this name for Deity as also
being feminine. The truth is that, as with the previous synonyms
for God, both sexes can express Love. No human is locked out of the
door to God as Love. The more we live the qualities emanating from
divine Love, the more we are expressing the image and likeness of
Elohim, whether male or female.

Some men have trouble accepting Elohim as divine Love because
many of the qualities listed below appear to be more feminine than
masculine and because this factor causes conflicts in macho-
minded men. Men are supposed to be able to express all the
qualities of God, but how can machismo be reconciled with what
machismo feels are lesser feminine qualities? Such a reconciliation
might diminish a man's machismo, which he often confuses with
manhood. Yet Jesus was not only masculine, overturning the tables
of the money-exchangers in the Jerusalem temple and later facing
the most painful form of torture unto death, but was also gentle,
kind, loving, compassionate to men, women, and children. His
expression of feminine qualities did not diminish his manhood but
heightened it with a supreme sense of balance.

So let us look at some of these qualities: affection, allegiance,
ardor, attentiveness, bliss, brotherhood, charity, Christly love,
compassion, consideration, cooperation, correction (acceptance
of), courtesy, devotion, emotional stability, empathy, faithfulness,

fatherhood (non-patriarchic), fearlessness, forgiveness, friendliness, generosity, gentleness, goodness, grace, harmlessness, humility, impartiality, inoffensiveness, kindness, listening, loyalty, meekness, mercy, mildness, moderation, modesty, motherhood (non-matriarchic), non-iniquity, obedience, parenthood (expressing the fullness of Abba as explained earlier), patience, politeness, protection (giving it and receiving it), respectfulness, sense of liberty, service, sincerity, sisterhood, spiritual love, sweetness, sympathy, tenderness, thoughtfulness, tolerance, unfeigned love (2 Corinthians 6:6), unselfishness, and so on through infinity. Cannot both sexes harvest the fields of divine Love, reaping the qualities of Love?

## God as Soul

Elohim not only has had to face down the idea of an anthropomorphic god. A pantheistic Greek philosophical god evolved known by the expression, "God is the soul of the world." Marcus Varro (116-27? BCE), a Roman scholar and writer, along with others, brought this philosophy to Rome. There are various presentations of this philosophical god, but the following is a fair, basic one. First, Zeus, then his counterpart, Jupiter or Jove, is seen as enveloping all the gods. His body is the world. Everything, even rocks and animals, as well as people, has a soul. All these souls make up the soul of the world and become God's soul. This soul can also be expanded to include the stars and planets, each of which in turn has its own individual soul. Thus the world is the body and soul of God.

The Englishman William Gilbert (1540-1603) had his doctorate in physics but was also known as a physician and cosmologist. In his *On the Loadstone*, Gilbert saw worms, roaches, moths, ants, plants, and morels (edible mushrooms) all "ennobled by soul," which makes up the soul of God. Similar to Varro, Gilbert went a step further, enveloping the sun and stars in his soul of the world.[71]

Another Englishman, William Harvey (1578-1657), earned his M.D. In his work *Animal Generation*, he attributed the mating of the cock and the hen to generating power of God as "the soul of the world."[72]

In his *Principles of Psychology*, Chapter XXI, "The Perception of Reality," the Irishman turned American, William James (1842-1910), wrote in the section of that chapter called "Belief in Objects of Theory," the italics being William's:

> *The perfect object of belief would be a God or "Soul of the World," represented both optimistically and moralistically (if such a combination could be), and withal so definitely conceived as to show us why our phenomenal experiences should be sent to us by Him in just the very way in which they come.*[73]

A few lines down, William James claimed that "the World-soul" sent him phenomena so that he might react upon them.

Whereas the above writers advocate the ancient idea of God as "the soul of the world," hints of this Greek philosophy can be found in the treatment of nature by the British romantic poets of the early nineteenth century and by the American transcendentalists, as well as in the blockbuster movie *Avatar*.

In his *City of God*, St. Augustine addressed this Greek philosophy in the fourth century. He first summarized some of the ideas involving Jove[74] and later skeptically summarized Varro's writings on the subject.[75] Eight hundred years later, Thomas Aquinas attacked this philosophy in his *Summa Theologica*:

> It was the opinion of some that every being is a body, and consequently some seem to have thought that there were no incorporeal substances except as united to bodies; so much so that some even held that "God is the soul of the world," as Augustine tells us. ... This is contrary to Catholic Faith, which asserts that God is exalted above all things, according to Psalm 8: 2: *Thy magnificence is exalted beyond the heavens.* ...[76]

Perhaps one of the greatest attackers of this Greek philosophy and champion of God as Elohim, without actually calling Him Elohim, was the famous mathematician and scientist, Sir Isaac Newton (1642-1727). In his *Mathematical Principles*, Newton not only lambasted this particular Greek philosophy but also any notion that God can be anthropomorphic:

This Being governs all things, not as the soul of the world, but as Lord over all; and on account of his dominion [Newton did not capitalize pronouns referring to God] he is wont [accustomed] to be called *Lord God* παντοκράτωρ, or *Universal Ruler* [although Newton used the term *Lord God*, he is not referring to an anthropomorphic being as evidenced in the Greek word he used, meaning absolute, universal Almighty, Omnipotence with dominion]; for *God* is a relative word, and has a respect to servants; and *Deity* is the dominion of God not over his own body, as those imagine who fancy God to be the soul of the world, but over servants. The Supreme God is a Being eternal, infinite, absolutely perfect; but a being, however perfect, without dominion, cannot be said to be Lord God; for we say, my God, your God, the God of *Israel*, the God of Gods, and Lord of Lords; but we do not say, my Eternal, your Eternal, the Eternal of *Israel*, the Eternal of Gods; we do not say, my Infinite, or my Perfect: these are titles which have no respect to servants. The word *God* usually signifies *Lord*; but every lord is not a God. It is the dominion of a spiritual being which constitutes a God: a true, supreme, or imaginary dominion makes a true, supreme, or imaginary [that is, imaginable, conceivable] God. And from his true dominion it follows that the true God is a living, intelligent, and powerful Being; and, from his other perfections, that he is supreme, or most perfect. He is eternal and infinite, omnipotent and omniscient; that is, his duration reaches from eternity to eternity; his presence from infinity to infinity; he governs all things, and knows all things that are or can be done. He is not eternity and infinity, but eternal and infinite; he is not duration or space, but he endures and is present. He endures forever, and is every where present; and, by existing always and every where, he constitutes duration or space. ... God is the same God, always and every where. He is omnipresent not *virtually* only, but also *substantially*; for virtue cannot subsist without substance. ... He is utterly void of all body and bodily figure, and can therefore neither be seen, nor heard, nor touched; nor ought he to be worshiped under the representation of any corporeal thing.[77]

Was Sir Isaac Newton, having written the above in his *Mathematical Principles*, presenting Elohim as a divine, eternal, infinite Principle? If so, he would have been in agreement with Thomas Aquinas, who wrote that "God is the principle of all being."[78]

For those who can accept Elohim as a divine, eternal, infinite Principle, the image and likeness of this advanced recognition of Elohim is subject to a sense of law far above the human sense of law and offers to him or her a wider sphere of qualities equally available for any individual who reaches out and truly demonstrates them, not as manifested in a mortal or human mind, but as the natural outcome inherent in the divine Mind of the universe: absoluteness (of truth), accomplishment, accuracy, advancement, alignment, assurance, authority (with divine guidance), availability, causation (with divine guidance), certainty, constancy, continuity, control (of oneself and one's circumstances), conviction, creativeness, demonstration, dependableness, diligence, discipline, dominion, effectiveness, efficiency, enforcement, *equality*, eternity (in the divine Mind), ethics, exactness, excellence, fairness, fixedness, force (with love), governance, guidance, harmony, indestructibleness of one's spiritual self, infinity (in the divine Principle), justice, law and rule, non-variableness (from the divine), obedience, omnipresence (availability of principle), order, organization, operation, perfection (*not* perfectionism), permanency (of the spiritual), precision, promptness, punctuality, purpose, regularity, regulation, reliability, security, stability, steadfastness, structure, trustworthiness, unchangeableness, and so on throughout infinity. Cannot both men and women labor in the harvest fields of infinite Principle, reaping the qualities of Principle?

The following quote is taken from Chapter 70 on Principle in the syntopicon of Britannica's *Great Books*:

"We need not go seeking any other Principles [other than three cosmic principles]," writes Plotinus. "This—the One and the Good—is our First, next to it follows the Intellectual Principle, the Primal Thinker, and upon this follows Soul. Such is the order in nature. The intellectual realm allows no more than these and no fewer. Those who hold to fewer Principles must hold the identity of either Intellectual Principle and Soul, or of Intellectual Principle and The First. ... To increase the Primals by making the Supreme Mind engender the Reason-Principle, and this again engender in the Soul a distinct power to act as mediator between Soul and the Supreme Mind, this is to deny intellection to the Soul, which would no longer derive its Reason from the Intellectual Principle, but from an intermediate. ... Therefore, we must affirm no more than these three Primals."

In the sense in which Plotinus conceives the three primals, they are not only principles in the order of reality, but are themselves the ultimate grades or modes of reality.[79]

Although Plotinus's logic is appealing, especially if his three primal principles were viewed as the One Principle with three aspects, there is a major flaw in his presentation according to Christians. Plotinus was a third-century Roman philosopher who had accepted Plato's idea of Soul as being the Soul of the World, a concept, you may recall, repeatedly condemned by Christian theologians. So is there a Christian concept of God as Soul, and if so, what effect would that have on our understanding of the equality of women? Let us examine the issues.

You may remember from earlier in this chapter that it is reasoned, since God is omniscient (all-knowing) and omnipresent, then His mind also must be omnipresent to be all-knowing, and thus God and His mind are the same essence; that is, God is Mind. Along these same lines of reasoning, we might conclude that God and His soul are also the same essence; that is, God is Soul. However, in my search through Christian literature I found no such references before the early part of the nineteenth century, only references from those who accepted or condemned the ancient, pagan idea of God being the Soul of the World; that is, that God's Soul is the collection of all the souls of all the grains of sand, all the souls of all the leaves, all the souls of insects, all the souls of the animals—in short, of every object, animal, and person. All these souls combined made up the pagan God as the Soul of the World. The reader may remember that St. Augustine condemned this idea in the fourth century, as did Thomas Aquinas eight hundred years later. And we just read a few pages back Sir Isaac Newton's condemnation of such a notion. Apparently, Christian writers avoided calling God Soul for fear of being misinterpreted as adopting the pagan idea of "God is the Soul of the World."

As the idea that God is the Soul of the World has become lost to thought, slowly the door was opening to accepting a non-pagan concept of God as Soul. The first such reference that I found came in the early nineteenth century. It can be found in William Wordsworth's poem "The Prelude; or, Growth of a Poet's Mind." Since Wordsworth was a British romantic nature poet, he is not above suspect of embracing the ancient Greek Soul-of-the-World idea. However, his choice of words appears more Christian than mythological:

> Wisdom and Spirit of the universe!
> Thou Soul that art the eternity of thought,
> ... (Book First, lines 400, 401)

Are there any more references? To start my search, I turned to unabridged dictionaries. The most comprehensive one is *The Oxford English Dictionary.* I used the compact edition, a micrographical reproduction of the complete text compiled from 1884-1908. Although three full pages were devoted to defining *soul,* I found no reference to God being Soul.

So I came across the ocean to Noah Webster's original *An American Dictionary of the English Language,* first published in 1828. Humanly speaking, Webster related soul to vital principle, spirit, life, power, intelligence, but he did not combine them all in a single divine sense. Some were granted some form of divinity, but only spirit is equated to God as when he defined *God* in part as "the eternal and infinite spirit," quoting Jesus' words "God is a spirit" in John 4.

Then George and Charles Merriam obtained the rights to Webster's dictionary and published it as an unabridged, revised, and enlarged "New Pictorial Edition." Webster's definition of *soul* appears to be untouched. What caught my eye was an appendix that included many thousands of new words and definitions since Webster wrote the original. However, the idea that God is Soul was not to be found in any American unabridged dictionary as of 1860.

As best I can tell, "God is Soul" first appeared in an unabridged dictionary in 1934, in *Webster's New International Dictionary of the English Language*, second edition. The idea was repeated in the third edition in 1966 and spotted again in the 1996 *Webster's New Universal Unabridged Dictionary*, deluxe edition, revised and updated, printed by Barnes and Noble and based on the second edition of *The Random House Dictionary of the English Language*. Research shows that since the late eighteen hundreds the Church of Christ, Scientist, has recognized God as Soul. At last, with the old pagan idea of God being the Soul of the World waning, as well as fear of being thought pagan instead of Christian, someone has let logic prevail for those who are looking for a greater understanding of Elohim and the nature of God's image and likeness. But does anyone else accept this idea of God being Soul?

I had heard that much of Christianity today has accepted the idea that God is Soul, Soul is God. So, to get a feel for this, I Googled the words "God is Soul." To my surprise, I received 52,100 results. Of course, some results really did not have anything to do with what I was researching; some talked about God being soul-food, for example. Some atheists declared that, since there is no universal god, there is no universal soul. A small few results claimed that the term "God is Soul" is well grounded now in Christianity, Judaism, and Islam. I have not researched this claim in Judaism and Islam, but certainly most of these thousands of contributors were Christians. Many were obviously very sincere but not good at putting their ideas in writing. We must remember that whether a person is sincere or not, believes that God is Soul or not, anyone can put anything on the internet. But many of these results were from various church websites of different denominations. Most were from individuals. One result stood out to me as perhaps what most were trying to say. The writer has an essay title "WHO AND WHAT IS GOD?" Several paragraphs down, the writer switches to all capitals in the answer: "WELL, TO BEGIN, GOD IS SOUL, AND SOUL IS GOD. NOT THE SOUL THAT IS IN CREATED MAN, BUT THE SOUL THAT IS DEITY AND SELF-EXISTENT, WITHOUT BEGINNING OR ENDING, AND WHOSE ENTITY IS THE ONE GREAT FACT IN THE UNIVERSE OF BEING."[80]

If this concept is acceptable, what are some of the Soul qualities expressible by both men and women? Here are few to consider: agility, balance, beauty, calmness, cleanliness, compatibility, composure, creativity, elasticity, expression, eloquence, emotional stability, grace, graciousness, harmony, holiness, joy, identity, immortality (of spiritual self), individuality, innocence, inspiration, morality, musicality, nobility, peace, perfection, poise, purity, rhythm, self-control, serenity, sinlessness, spiritual sense, stillness, sweetness, tranquility, uniqueness, and so on through infinity. Cannot both sexes labor in the harvest fields of Soul, reaping the qualities of Soul?

\* \* \*

With two different concepts of God in the Old Testament and with the views toward women varying according to which concept of God society generally accepts, at least five ironies have evolved.

**Irony #1.** Thomas Aquinas reasoned that "God is not a body"[81] and consequently that God's image and likeness is not a body: "It is according to his intelligence and reason, which are incorporeal, that man is said to be according to the image of God."[82] This might explain the image and likeness to God as Mind, but as shown earlier in this chapter, God has also been claimed to be Life, Spirit, Truth, Love, Principle, Soul, most of which Aquinas also included in his writings. In any case, here he saw the image and likeness as not having a body but as being the expression of God's qualities.

Furthermore, Aquinas, in discussing "the eternity of God," had this to say:

> As God, although incorporeal, is named in Scripture metaphorically by corporeal names, so eternity though simultaneously whole, is called by names implying time and succession.[83]

Most of the writers quoted in this chapter probably would agree with Aquinas on this point. The irony is this: After describing a non-anthropomorphic Elohim as the Supreme Being, why do these masculine writers then turn around and switch from Elohim and His image and likeness, both male and female, as explained in Genesis 1, to the metaphor of an anthropomorphic Lord God in Genesis 2 with only the male being the image and likeness of God and the female being the image and likeness of either the serpent or the image and likeness of a man's rib?

The age-old question has been, which came first, the chicken or the egg? Religious society reasoned before eggs were discovered in women in the nineteenth century that since humans don't have eggs, then naturally the chicken, that is Adam, came first. Woman was an afterthought, a gift to man. In contrast to a gift, some even break the word *woman* into two syllables and, with *wo* being a variant of *woe*, say that *wo-man* means, "Woe is man!" Some religious leaders in the past, and perhaps a few even today, see woman as partially the image and likeness of Adam, woman being a misbegotten man, having never fully developed into a man. After describing God in accordance to Genesis 1, why, when it comes to the image and likeness, do so many male theologians switch from Genesis 1 to Genesis 2?

**Irony #2.** Why would such great thinkers and Christian theologians like Albert the Great and Thomas Aquinas turn to a pagan Greek philosopher like Aristotle for their views of women instead of to Christ? Why do theologians today still hang on to these conclusions whose syllogisms have been proven faulty? Quoting Aristotle, Aquinas concluded that women were not fit for the priesthood. Why are these ancient myths still considered sacred?

**Irony #3.** The examination of this irony is not meant, as mentioned in a previous chapter, as a condemnation of the gay community but as a critique of theological inconsistencies.

Why was it in the eleventh and twelfth centuries that, although sensuality was the cause of impurity, sexual relationships between men and women were considered impure, but sexual relationships among monks and priests were officially tolerated? During this time, homosexual poetry and other writings flourished. For example, Anselm, a monk and archbishop of Canterbury, wrote plainly and openly of his physical love of a man, as did also the English Abbot Ailred of Rievaulx, who put it all in Christian context.[84]

Yes, the acceptance of homosexuality attributed to Plato could have entered Christianity with Augustine's Christianizing that Greek philosopher's ideas some centuries earlier. But could there also have been some theological basis? Was it thought all right to have sexual relationships between a man made in the image and likeness of the Lord God and another man also made in the image and likeness of an anthropomorphic Lord God, but it was sin to have a relationship between a man made in the image and likeness of the Lord God and an impure, imperfect woman made in the image and likeness either of a serpent or of a man's rib? Was this tolerance of sex among priests and monks another case of the clergy's accepting the all-male image and likeness implied in Genesis 2 and 3 and either overlooking or rejecting the dual male-and-female image and likeness of Elohim stated in the first chapter? Could this man-with-man-only philosophy have evolved to check those clergymen who had been having promiscuous sex with women? Where were purity and spirituality of thought for clergymen supposed to fit into the idea of godliness? Was God secretly viewed as a sexual being as was Zeus?

**Irony #4.** Since even in anthropomorphic creation the Lord God gave Eve to Adam as a helpmate, why then exclude from men the Lord God's gift? As for lack of purity, was the problem with the women, or in the minds of men who could not control their thoughts? If the latter, why is it that half of humanity is abused and ostracized because the members of the other half cannot control their thinking and their ability not to be led like Adam into temptation?

**Irony #5.** In Matthew 19, we read:

4 And he [Jesus] answered and said unto them, Have ye not read, that he which made them at the beginning made them male and female,

5 And said, For this cause shall a man leave father and mother, and shall cleave to his wife: and they twain shall be one flesh?

6 Wherefore they are no more twain, but one flesh. ...

In these verses, Jesus appears to be emphasizing that marriage is a unit, a unity, a commitment to express between the twain a oneness in the vast qualities of divine Love. There is no hint of the theological view that the male is the only and the female is just an entity to be controlled or maybe even eliminated because she descended from the serpent goddess. Notice that Jesus referred back to Elohim and His image and likeness, male and female, in Genesis 1 and to the two becoming one flesh in Genesis 2. They both become one because they both are committed to being one with divine Love.

Is it not ironic how superstitions, misunderstandings of the biology of women, and even arrogance, have reduced woman from equality in this state of oneness to one of inferiority and subordination, to be manipulated and worked, in many cases, like a horse on a farm?

* * *

St. Paul wrote the Romans (9:8): "They which are the children of the flesh, these are not the children of God." Can it be then that no mortal is the image and likeness of immortal Mind, Spirit, Truth, Love, but as each individual lives a higher form of humanity, he or she is manifesting the image and likeness to the degree that he or she is being present with the Spirit and absent from the body, as St. Paul put it, that is, living the substantive qualities of Mind, Spirit, Truth, Love? According to the third chapter of Colossians, Paul told us that, as we control our anger, not be hateful or cruel, nor lie to one another (verses 8 and 9), then we are "now a new person..., becoming more and more like [our] Creator," to use the Contemporary English translation, or more like "the image of him that created" us, to use the King James' (verse 10). The qualities manifested in this image are "mercies, kindness, humbleness of mind, meekness, longsuffering; forbearing one another, and forgiving one another, if any man have a quarrel against any" (verses 12 and 13). Cannot women, as well as men, express these qualities and thus become a new person, more and more like the creator, more like the image of Elohim who created us?

After all, we read in Isaiah (2:22), "Cease ye from man, whose breath is in his nostrils: for wherein is he to be accounted of?" a clear reference to Jehovah's creation of Adam, "and breathed into his nostrils the breath of life" (Genesis 2:7). The Psalmist prayed, "As for me, I will behold thy face in righteousness: I shall be satisfied, when I awake, with thy likeness" (Psalms 17:15). Thus the person whose breath is in his or her nostrils is *not* this likeness, but is in a sleeping state, from which when awakened, will see him- or herself in God's likeness. And how does one awake? By seeing oneself as the reflection of God in righteousness. The only way of seeing ourselves as God's likeness is by living the qualities of Elohim, in this case, according to David, by beholding the Infinite in righteousness. Cannot women, as well as men, awake in this righteousness and behold the source of their identity?

Paul reworded David's thought: "...we all, with open face beholding as in a glass the glory of the Lord, are changed into the same image from glory to glory, even as by the Spirit of the Lord" (II Corinthians 3:18). What does it take to see the "the glory of the

Lord" in a spiritual mirror and thus be changed, from that whose breath is in his or her nostrils, into the same image in the mirror? A miracle? Or reformation in accordance with grace? Jesus answered these questions with one of his beatitudes: "Blessed are the pure in heart: for they shall see God" (Matthew 5:8). Who dare say that a woman cannot reform as well as a man or even better and thus see her spiritual image in the mirror of Spirit? The arrogant or patriarchic? Who dare say that a spiritual, feminine image of divine Love is inferior to the masculine? The arrogant or patriarchic?

"No!" cry those who believe in an all-male God. "Blasphemy! Women cannot be the image and likeness of God because men are the sole image and therefore the only contributor to offspring. Women are punished for misguiding Jehovah's image and likeness and, therefore, must suffer in their menstrual cycles and in birthing because of their sins in the Garden of Eden. It does not matter that human eggs were not discovered until the early part of the nineteenth century. We believe what we have always believed because our theology is sacred. Blasphemy!"

Yet the syllogisms based upon Aristotle's concept of women and upon the superstitions and misunderstandings in the anthropomorphic sections of the Scriptures have had all their major premises proven wrong about women, dissolved into nothingness! With the major premises gone, shouldn't the conclusions based on these false premises—based on nothingness—be open to scrutiny? Just because an ancient idea has been held onto for so long, does it make that idea true?

Of course, there are differences between the sexes. There has to be for reproduction and a mother's instinct, for example. But it has been the priority of patriarchy to focus on these differences. You can spot a patriarchic person or institution by his or its *focus* on the differences between the sexes. However, when patriarchy and all its ingrained influences are set aside, actuality reveals an alternate reality. One of the points of Allan K. Johnson's excellent book, *The Gender Knot*, is that we need to focus on actuality, the vast sameness of the human genders. Focusing on Elohim rather than an all-male God is the first step. Recognizing that all the qualities of Elohim are open to all, males and females alike, is the second step. Cultivating and living these qualities of the image and likeness is the third and essential step.

Some women may manifest the image and likeness in their lives better than men do, and vice versa. It's not the gender but the commitment of the individual to better him- or herself that draws one closer to the Life that is Elohim.

Patriarchy teaches that Providence has given mortal men the right to control and dominate women. Non-patriarchic existence teaches that the infinite Mind of the universe controls and loves all, all of Elohim's image and likeness, both male and female. The all-seeing eye of divine Mind recognizes the full significance of all the masculine and feminine qualities, the vast nature of Elohim. Those mortals who crave power and control are usurping the power and controlling influences of God, thus making themselves out as gods and violating the First Commandment, "Thou shalt have no other gods before me" (Exodus 20:3).

Where do ancient, superstitious, mythological concepts of God differ from Truth? The closer humanity comes in this differentiation, the closer we will find our concept of God actually overlapping or correlating with Truth. And the better our understanding of God, the better we can grasp our true selves—both male and female— made in the image and likeness of Mind, of Spirit, of Love. We may never completely grasp the allness of Omniscience, whose ideas are ever expanding and multiplying throughout the universe—not in space, but in infinity—not in time, but in the nowness of eternity.

Can that ancient, bearded God of wisdom depicted on the ceiling of the Sistine Chapel be this Allness, this ALL-in-all?

Perhaps some males feel closer to the anthropomorphic Lord God Jehovah, but any person—either male or female—is as close to Elohim as the individual manifests or lives the qualities of Elohim. The sex of the individual—contrary to old theology's masculine teachings—is irrelevant to expressing the image and likeness of Elohim. Yes, as humans, males may find some qualities easier to express than females do, and females find other qualities easier to manifest than males can, but all qualities are open to all to make their own. To say otherwise, is it not to be arrogant?

Here are a few questions for my Christian brethren: Can we witness the transformation of an individual without that individual's continuously expressing more and more of these qualities radiating from the various synonyms of Elohim? Can this be what Paul meant when he wrote, "Be ye transformed by the renewing of your mind"? (See Romans 12:2.) Can one really be born again without living more of Elohim's qualities? Can one be truly born again if he thinks God radiates only half the good qualities of infinity? Look again at what Jesus said to Nicodemus, a ruler of the Jews: "That which is born of the flesh is flesh [the sons of Jehovah's Adam]; and that which is born of the Spirit is spirit [the Christly children of Elohim]" (John 3:6). Can it be that in this human experience both genders are equal before God, equally loved by divine Love?

As the understanding of Elohim extends, the freedom of women expands.

# Endnotes
## Chapter 5

1   *The Interpreter's Dictionary of the Bible*, vol. 2 of 5, Nashville: Abingdon Press, 1962, pp. 413, 414.

2   Herman Melville, *Moby Dick; or, The Whale*, chap. 132, Chicago: William Benton, 1952, pp, 394-395. [republished from 1851]

3   William Shakespeare, *Macbeth*, act 1, sc. 5, 1. 42.

4   Gregory, Bishop of Nyssa, *On the Making of Man*, ques. V, par. 2, in *Nicene and Post-Nicene Fathers*, 2nd series, vol. 5 of 14, Peabody, MA: Hendrickson Publishers, 1995, p. 391. [republished from 1892]

5   St. Augustine, *The City of God*, chaps. 17, 23, 24, Chicago: William Benton, 1952, pp. 353, 358. [republished translation by Marcus Dods (1834-1909)]

6   John of Damascus, *Exposition of the Orthodox Faith*, chap. XII, par. 4, in *Nicene and Post-Nicene Fathers*, 2nd series, vol. 9 of 14, Peabody, MA: Hendrickson Publishers, 1995, p. 14. [republished from 1892]

7   Thomas Aquinas, *Summa Theologica*, Pt. I, ques. 18, art.4, trans. by Fathers of the English Dominican Province, London: Burns, Oates & Washbourne, 1915-1922.

8   Dante Alighieri, *The Inferno*, trans. John Ciardi, canto XI, line 90, New York: The New American Library, 1954, p. 106.

9   Dante Alighieri, *Paradise*, canto XXVI, lines 100-120, in *The Divine Comedy of Dante Alighieri*, Chicago: William Benton, 1952, p.148. [republished translation by Charles Eliot Norton (1827-1908)]

10  René Descartes, *Objections against the Meditations and Replies*, reply to 2nd set of obj., point 2, par. 11, Chicago: William Benton, 1952, p, 122. [republished translation by Elizabeth S. Haldane and G. R. T. Ross for Cambridge University Press, 1931]

11  Benedict de Spinoza, *Ethics,* part I, prop. 17, Chicago: William Benton, 1952, p. 363. [republished translation by W. H. White (1831-1913) and revised by A. H. Stirling (19th cen. translator)]

12  Spinoza, part II, prop. 1, p. 374.

13  John Locke, *Concerning Human Understanding*, bk. IV, chap. X, sec. 12, 13, 16, 18, 19, Chicago: William Benton, 1952, pp. 352-354. [republished from the sixteen hundreds]

14 James Hastings, *Dictionary of the Bible*, New York: Charles Scribner's Sons, 1937, p. 935.

15 For example, see Mary Baker Eddy, *Science and Health with Key to the Scriptures*, Boston: Trustees under the Will of Mary Baker G. Eddy, 1906, 1934, p. 591.

16 Thornton Wilder, *Three Plays: Thornton Wilder*, New York: Bantam Books, 1957, p. 28.

17 Paul Lee Tan, *The Interpretation of Prophecy*, Winona Lake, IN: BMH Books, 1974, p. 213.

18 See DVD *What tHe βLεεP Dθ w∑ (K) ow!?*, 2004.

19 See http://cosmos.asu.edu/publications/books/mind_god.htm.

20 Paul Davies, *The Mind of God: The Scientific Basis for a Rational World*, New York: Simon and Schuster, 1992, p. 232.

21 See the DVD *Unlocking the Mystery of Life*, Illustra Media, 2002.

22 *Ibid.*

23 *Ibid.*

24 *Ibid.*

25 *Ibid.*

26 *Ibid.*

27 Allan G. Johnson, *The Gender Knot: Unraveling Our Patriarchal Legacy*, Philadelphia: Temple University Press, 2005, pp. 84, 85, 96, 97.

28 This list of qualities and those to follow have been generated by recommendations from several friends.

29 Plotinus, *Third Ennead*, chap. VII, sec 5, Chicago: William Benton, 1952, pp. 121-122. [republished translation (originally 1917-1930) by Stephen MacKenna and B. S. Page]

30 St. Augustine, *Confessions*, bk. I, chap. VI, Chicago: William Benton, 1952, p. 3. [republished translation by Edward B. Pusey (1800-1882)]

31 St. Augustine, *Confessions*, bk. VII, chap. I, sec. 2, p. 43.

32 Aquinas, 1st part, ques. 18, art. 3 ("I answer that").

33 *Ibid.*, reply to obj. 2.

34 *Ibid.*, art. 4, ("I answer that").

35 *Ibid.*, (reply to obj. 2).

36 David F. Noble, *A World Without Women*, New York: Alfred A. Knopf, 1992, p. 285.

37 Johnson, pp. 84, 85.

38 *The Oxford English Dictionary, The Compact Edition*, vol. II, New York: Oxford University Press, 1971, p. 2967.

39  St. Bazil, *On the Spirit*, chap. IX, in *Nicene and Post-Nicene Fathers*, 2nd series, vol. 8 of 14, Peabody, MA: Hendrickson Publishers, 1995, p. 15. [republished from 1892]

40  St. Gregory Nazinanzen, "On the Holy Spirit" as *The Fifth Theological Oration*, sec. XII, in *Nicene and Post-Nicene Fathers*, 2nd series, vol. 7 of 14, Peabody, MA: Hendrickson Publishers, 1995, p.321. [republished from 1892]

41  St. Ambrose, *Of the Holy Spirit*, bk. I, chap. VII, sec. 82, in *Nicene and Post-Nicene Fathers*, 2nd series, vol. 10 of 14, Peabody, MA: Hendrickson Publishers, 1995, p.104. [republished from 1892]

42  Ambrose, chap. XV, sec. 171, on p. 113.

43  St. Jerome, *Letter* LVIII, sec. 3, in *Nicene and Post-Nicene Fathers*, 2nd series, vol. 6 of 14, Peabody, MA: Hendrickson Publishers, 1995, p.120. [republished from 1892]

44  John of Damascus, chap. XII, par. 4, p. 14.

45  Richard Trench, *The Parables of Our Lord*, London: Macmillan, 1882, p. 254.

46  Joan Chamberlain Engelsman, *The Feminine Dimension of the Divine*, Wilmette, IL: Chiron, 1987, pp. 37, 81, 112, 117, 127, 142, 152.

47  Athanasius, *Defence Before Constantius*, sec. 12, in *Nicene and Post-Nicene Fathers*, 2nd series, vol. 4 of 14, Peabody, MA: Hendrickson Publishers, 1995, p.242. [republished from 1892]

48  St. Bazil, chap. XIX, sec. 48, on p. 30.

49  St. Augustine, *Confessions*, bk. III, sec. VI, par. 10, on p. 15.

50  St. Augustine, bk. V, sec. III, par. 5, on p. 28.

51  St. Augustine, bk. VII, Sec. X, par. 16, on p. 48.

52  St. Augustine, bk. VII, sec. XV, par. 21, on p. 50.

53  St. Augustine, bk. VII, sec. XVII, par. 23, p. 50.

54  St. Augustine, bk. XI, sec. III, par. 5, on p. 90.

55  Aquinas, 1st part, ques. 2 art. 2, obj. 3 and reply to obj. 3.

56  Aquinas, 1st part, ques. 16, art. 5, "Whether God is Truth?"

57  Dante Alighieri, *Paradise*, canto II, sec. beginning with l. 31, on p. 108.

58  Georg Wilhelm Friedrick Hegel, "The German World," *Philosophy of History*, sec. III, "The Modern Time," chap. I, "The Reformation," par. 5, Chicago: William Benton, 1952, p. 349. [republished translation of 1858 by J. Sibree, rev. 1899]

59  Garry Wills, *Papal Sin: Structures of Deceit*, New York: Doubleday, 2000, pp. 109-110, 120.

60 Gregory of Nyssa, *On the Making of Man*, sec. V, in *Nicene and Post-Nicene Fathers*, 2nd series, vol. 5 of 14, Peabody, MA: Hendrickson Publishers, 1995, p.391. [republished from 1892]

61 Gregory of Nyssa, *On the Soul and the Resurrection*, on p. 450.

62 John Cassian, *First Conference of Abbot Joseph, chap. XIII, sent. 1-2*, in *Conferences*, in *Nicene and Post-Nicene Fathers*, 2nd series, vol. 11 of 14, Peabody, MA: Hendrickson Publishers, 1995, p.454. [republished from 1892]

63 St. Augustine, *Confessions*, bk. VII, sec. X, par. 16, on p. 48.

64 Aquinas, 1st part, ques. 20, art. 1.

65 Aquinas, ques. 37, art. 1.

66 Aquinas, ques. 74, art. 3.

67 Dante Alighieri, *The Inferno (Hell)*, canto I, l. 37, in *The Divine Comedy of Dante Alighieri*, Chicago: William Benton, 1952, p.1. [republished translation by Charles Eliot Norton (1827-1908)]

68 Dante Alighieri, *Purgatory*, canto III, l. 133, in *The Divine Comedy of Dante Alighieri*, Chicago: William Benton, 1952, p.57. [republished translation by Charles Eliot Norton (1827-1908)]

69 Dante, *Paradise*, canto XXXII, l. 139, on p. 156.

70 Leo Tolstoy, *War and Peace*, bk. 12, chap. XVI, Chicago: William Benton, 1952, p. 561. [republished translation by Louise Maude (1855-1939) and Aylmer Maude (1858-1938)]

71 William Gilbert, *On the Loadstone*, bk. 5th, chap. 12, Chicago: William Benton, 1952, p. 105. [republished translation by P. Fleury Mottelay in 1893]

72 William Harvey, *Animal Generation*, exerc. 50, Chicago: William Benton, 1952, p. 427.
[republished translation by Robert Willis in 1847]

73 William James, *Principles of Psychology*, chap. XXI, Chicago: William Benton, 1952, 658.

74 St. Augustine, *City of God*, bk. IV, chap. 11, on pp. 194-196.

75 St. Augustine, bk. VII, chap. 6, on p. 248.

76 Aquinas, 1st part, ques. 51, art. 1, reply to obj. 1.

77 Isaac Newton, *The Principia: Mathematical Principles of Natural Philosophy*, bk. III: "The System of the World," sec. titled "General Scholium," 3rd ed., 1726 [trans. by André Motte in 1729].

78 Aquinas, part I, ques. 3, art. 5.

79 *The Great Ideas: A Syntopicon of Great Books of the Western World*, vol. II, Chicago: William Benton, 1952, p. 422.

80 http://www.divinelove.org/WHO-AND-WHAT-IS-GOD-

81 Aquinas, art. 2.

82 Aquinas, art. 1.
83 Aquinas, ques. 10, art. 1.

For more than a thousand years, even long before Aquinas, Christian theologians "understood the image of God in humanity to be located in the possession of reason or rationality." See Karen Jo Torjesen, *When Women Were Priests*, New York: HarperOne, 1993, p. 239.

84 Noble, pp. 134, 135, 155, 172.

# EPILOGUE

Outside the spiritual realm, perhaps the one major constant of our modern age is change. This change awakens new truths in our thought. We then synthesize them with the proven ones of the past to bring humanity closer to Truth. With this process, humanity becomes less shackled.

A number of years ago a friend suggested that, in order for humanity to progress, mortals need to die and be replaced by other mortals with fewer prejudices, less ignorance, and fewer limited thoughts. What he was saying is that inhibition based in preconception is the enemy of humanity's progress and it often requires many generations to overcome the erroneous influences that are handed down with the good—many generations to replace the old, outdated notions proven false with new ideas more associated with truth and principle. That is not to say that all old—or even most old—ideas are outdated. One of the important lessons we learn from history is to reject that which was unprincipled and to duplicate that which has benefited humanity.

Not everyone is like Alabama's former Governor George Wallace, who first stood for segregation, even standing up to the Federal Government, but who later accepted integration, even becoming a champion of jobs for blacks. With knowledge running to and fro at an ever-increasing rate, with communications uniting the world under a new banner of increased tolerance and open-mindedness, we ought to find more and more people, institutions, and cultures cutting off the shackles of unwarranted prejudices and ignorance.

At the other end of the spectrum, new ideas based on syllogisms formed in the vacuum of historical facts and lessons can be just as dangerous to society as the old conclusions based on false syllogisms. A false syllogism is still a false syllogism, no matter whether it was formed in ancient times or during our present age. Take, for example, the criticism of former President Harry Truman

151

for ordering the atomic bombing of Hiroshima and Nagasaki to end World War II. The critics reveal their ignorance of history in their outrage. The fact was that the firebombing of Tokyo and other Japanese cities was already killing thousands of civilians and destroying their cities. Expecting an invasion, the Japanese had trained both their military and civilians—men, women, and children—to fight to the end like their heroic Kamikaze pilots. If they were going to be defeated, they were going to kill as many Americans as possible in the process. President Truman was advised that an invasion of Japan would kill many more civilians than two atomic bombs would, as well as an estimated 100,000 more American troops. Only after the two atomic bombs, when the Japanese believed that they were going to be defeated but the Americans were going to have no more casualties, did the Japanese become open-minded and accepted change. People should remember that a syllogism formed in the vacuum of historical facts and lessons is almost invariably going to be tainted, if not outright false.

Human nature resists change. This resistance to change is perhaps one of humanity's greatest weaknesses. Furthermore, one of the great ironies of humanity is that erroneous beliefs are often prolonged by superstitions, by misunderstandings, and, sometimes, by arrogance embodied in human institutions that claim to be the embodiment of *Truth.*

There are certain laws that are constant—the laws of physics, of chemistry, of mathematics—generally, many of the laws of nature. One possible exception may lie with physics, if singularity is found to exist in black holes or was the state of physical existence before the Big Bang. And all evidence points to singularity in black holes. Otherwise, what *is* changing is humanity's growing thought on how to use these laws to humanity's advantage. But are there also certain laws of divine Principle that are constant, changing humanity's growing thought of God, of the universe, of what makes up the image and likeness of God—as divine Mind sees the image, but not necessarily as humans have recognized it with all of humanity's ancient creeds, unproven hypotheses, and psychological hang-ups?

Say that two football teams arrive at the Super Bowl rated with an equal chance of winning. Although equal, the two come with different strengths and different weaknesses, with their various ups and downs during the season. Likewise, men and women come into the gender super bowl with their different strengths and their different weaknesses. The big difference between the football and gender super bowls is that, if men and women can emerge as diverse but equal players on the same team, they will win the super bowl of life.

The level of masculine stability in a society or culture can be measured by the level of feminine importance in the masculine thought. If there is a balance in importance, the masculine character is strong. But if the feminine is subdued, then the masculine macho is psychologically weaker and not as stable, even though men in their state of instability actually believe that they are the ones who are stable! Oh, the irony!

If we are to accept the masculine and feminine nature of God as discussed in Chapters 2, 3, and 5, then the degree to which a society or culture grasps the nature of Deity can be measured in part by the degree to which that society or culture recognizes the equality of men and women and of the masculine and feminine qualities. These qualities vary but essentially are the same. Can it be that they all are essential in the completeness of humanity, of spiritual existence, and of God?

To think that the past does not influence the present is to live in the Adamic mist with its confusing consequences. Collect all the ancient superstitions and fears pertaining to blood and the woman's menstruation, all the Aristotelian notions, prejudices, and arrogance about women and the influences of those on Christianity, all the general arrogance based upon the apparent psychological need to believe some others inferior, in this case women, so as to promote one's own self-esteem. Then stuff all these fascinations and falsehoods into a coffin and "nail" it shut with solidified, thus reinforced tampons.

Next, bury it with an opening-curse, all incased in a fifty-foot cube made of steel-reinforced cement. Drop the block into a hole at least fifty-six feet deep.

Let the eulogy with joyous tears begin!

Dust to dust.

As the dirt covers over the last remains, let the spiritual officiary read the words of Elohim: "So God created man in his own image, in the image of God created he him; male and female created he them. ... And God saw every thing that he had made, and, behold, it was very good" (Gen. 1: 27, 31).

Have the tombstone read:

Here lies
Nothingness

Ancient time – Now
May he rest in oblivion.

One of the defects of human nature is to look down on others so that we feel better about ourselves. The treatment of females in Africa, the Mideast, and Asia is obviously deplorable. But do Western men, at least in part, look down upon the developing nations' treatment of women so as to justify their own patriarchal culture as not being so bad? If the West is to lead by example, should not the Christians of the West cast their own patriarchic mote out of their own eye so as to better help our brothers and sisters of all faiths cast that deplorable mote out of their own eyes? If not, are we then hypocrites?

Since all the syllogisms based on superstitions, misunderstandings, and arrogance are built on false premises, why do their false conclusions still linger as though true? The conclusions drawn from faulty syllogisms are slowly going the way of the fallen, dead leaves swirling in the wind and being sucked toward that coffin of dust, like star dust sucked into a black hole. The minds that nurture them are being swept away with the dead leaves. Spending eternity stuffed with erroneous beliefs and buried in a fifty-foot cube of cement is not my vision of living in the heaven of Truth. The stench of decaying error would be horrible! To paraphrase the master poet, "To yield to truth, or not to yield to truth: that is the question."

The Law of Truth: Truth pounds error; any person or institution embracing the error also receives the pounding and eventually joins the dust carried away in the wind. To avoid the pounding, one must let go of the error. Denying the error and declaring the truth make up the first step of that process of repentance and healing in the human experience.

As quoted in Chapter Five, Thomas Aquinas reasoned that "it is according to his intelligence and reason, which are incorporeal, that man is said to be according to the image of God."[207] But there is more than intellect in the image and likeness of Elohim. From

Mind, Life, Spirit, Truth, Love, and, if acceptable to the reader, Principle and Soul, dozens upon dozens of qualities radiate. If St. Paul is correct that "there is neither male nor female: for ye are all one in Christ Jesus" (Galatians 3:28), then all these qualities are equally available for any individual to live the image and likeness of Elohim. What grace we find through Christ!

We had more than fifteen thousand years of rule by women, called matriarchy. As Endo-European, patriarchic culture slowly replaced the old European, feminine culture, a thousand years or so of transition began to strip women of their power and rights. As might be expected, Hebrew women resisted giving up their belief in a fertility goddess for an all-male Deity called Yahweh, or Jehovah. After the Exile, when Jehovah emerged a masculine-feminine God like Elohim, women finally let go of their fertility goddess.

Today, with varying views or understandings of the nature of Jehovah, Elohim—still that constant Being who had made man both male and female—has emerged as the one constant for a new age, an age that rules without favoring either sex or gender. A new word for this age is epicenarchy (gender-neutral rule).

Just as women tried to hold onto a remnant of matriarchy as patriarchy subdued them, we should expect there to be some men holding onto patriarchy as it too is replaced by epicenarchy. Human nature resists giving up material power, even if it is not deserved or warranted. Just as there was friction as matriarchy transitioned into patriarchy, the repetition of history teaches us that we should not be surprised to experience friction during the transition into epicenarchy. Some men will hold to their all-male Deity just as ancient women held to Asherah. Some women, as they find new-born freedom and rights, may adopt a Captain Ahab revenge on what they see are "the murderous thinkings" in all men. But the sooner we all accept the evidence and logic of Truth and the wisdom of the divine Mind, the sooner we all will be bowing before the open arms of divine Love. Then epicenarchy will have replaced patriarchy, and both men and women will have found a new sense of Spirit's freedom.

The light of Truth unveils the dark limitations of both matriarchy and patriarchy, pointing to epicenarchy as a higher manifestation of Elohim's rule, as a more just and fair form of governing humanity. The curtain has risen upon the dawning of a new age, an age slowly dismissing the conclusions based on false syllogisms rendered from superstitions, ignorance, and bias, slowly accepting the logical and emotional reasoning behind a higher sense of equality.

# Endnote
## Epilogue

1  Thomas Aquinas, *Summa Theologica*, part I, ques. 3, art.1, trans. by Fathers of the English Dominican Province, London: Burns, Oates & Washbourne, 1915-1922.

# BIBLIOGRAPHY

Ambrose, *Of the Holy Spirit*, in *Nicene and Post-Nicene Fathers*, 2nd series, vol. 10 of 14, Peabody, MA: Hendrickson Publishers, 1995. [republished from 1892]

*The Ante-Nicene Fathers*, tran. S. Thelwall, online at http://www. earlychristianwritings.com/text/tertullian22.html.

Aquinas, Thomas, *Summa Theologica*, trans. by Fathers of the English Dominican Province, London: Burns, Oates & Washbourne, 1915-1922.

Aristotle, *History of Animals*, in *The Works of Aristotle*, ed. by W. D. Ross, London: Oxford University Press, 1928.

Aristotle, *Nicomachean Ethics*, bk. VIII, chap. 10.

Aristotle, *On the Generation of Animals*, bk. II, chap. 3; bk. IV, chap. 2

Aristotle, *Metaphysics*, bk. VI, chap. 1.

Aristotle, *Politics*, bk. I, chap. 12.

Athanasius, *Defence Before Constantius*, sec. 12, in *Nicene and Post-Nicene Fathers*, 2nd series, vol. 4 of 14, Peabody, MA: Hendrickson Publishers, 1995. [republished from 1892]

St. Augustine, *The City of God*, Chicago: William Benton, 1952. [republished translation by Marcus Dods (1834-1909)]

St. Augustine, *Confessions*, Chicago: William Benton, 1952, [republished translation by Edward B. Pusey (1800-1882)]

St. Bazil, *On the Spirit*, chap. IX, in *Nicene and Post-Nicene Fathers*, 2nd series, vol. 8 of 14, Peabody, MA: Hendrickson Publishers, 1995. [republished from 1892]

Bristow, John Temple, *What Paul REALLY Said About Women: An Apostle's Liberating Views on Equality in Marriage, Leadership, and Love*, San Francisco: Harper, 1991.

Cassian, John, *First Conference of Abbot Joseph, chap. XIII, sent. 1-2*, in *Conferences*, in *Nicene and Post-Nicene Fathers*, Peabody, MA: Hendrickson Publishers, 1995. [republished from 1892]

https://cosmos.asu.edu/publication/mind-god

DVD *Unlocking the Mystery of Life*, Illustra Media, 2002.

DVD *What tHe βLεεP Dθ wΣ (K) ow!?*, 2004.

Dante Alighieri, *The Inferno*, trans. John Ciardi, canto XI, line 90, New York: The New American Library, 1954.

Dante Alighieri, *The Inferno (Hell)*, in *The Divine Comedy of Dante Alighieri*, Chicago: William Benton, 1952. [republished translation by Charles Eliot Norton (1827-1908)]

Dante Alighieri, *Paradise; Purgatory*, in *The Divine Comedy of Dante Alighieri*, Chicago: William Benton, 1952. [republished translation by Charles Eliot Norton (1827-1908)]

Davies, Paul, *The Mind of God: The Scientific Basis for a Rational World*, New York: Simon and Schuster, 1992.

de Spinoza, Benedict, *Ethics*, Chicago: William Benton, 1952. [republished translation by W. H. White (1831-1913) and revised by A. H. Stirling (19th cen. translator)]

Des Jardins, Julie, "The Passion of Madame Curie," *Smithsonian. com*, October 2011, pp. 82-90.

Descartes, René, *Objections against the Meditations and Replies*, Chicago: William Benton, 1952. [republished translation by Elizabeth S. Haldane and G. R. T. Ross for Cambridge University Press, 1931]

http://www.divinelove.org

Dummelow, J. R., *A Commentary on the Holy Bible*, New York: Macmillan, 1912.

Dummelow, J. R., *A Commentary on the Holy Bible*, Macmillan Publishing Co., New York, 1936.

Durant, Will, *Caesar and Christ*, New York: Simon and Schuster, 1944.

Eddy, Mary Baker, *Science and Health with Key to the Scriptures*, Boston: Trustees under the Will of Mary Baker G. Eddy, 1906, 1934.

Ehrman, Bart D., *Forged*, New York: HarperOne, 2011.

Ehrman, Bart D., *The Orthodox Corruption of Scripture: The Effect of Early Christological Controversies on the Text of the New Testament*, New York: Oxford University Press, 1993.

Eiselen, Frederick C., Edwin Lewis, and David G. Downey, *The Abington Bible Commentary*, New York: Abington Press, 1929, p. 288.

Engelsman, Joan Chamberlain, *The Feminine Dimension of the Divine*, Wilmette, IL: Chiron, 1987.

Furness, Dr. Robert, Telephonic interview on horse canines (Aristotle reference) about 2001.

Gilbert, William, *On the Loadstone*, Chicago: William Benton, 1952. [republished translation by P. Fleury Mottelay in 1893]

Gimbutas, Marija, *The Goddesses and Gods of Old Europe: 6500-3500 BC*, New and updated ed., Berkeley: University of California Press, 1982.

Gordon D. Fee, *The First Epistle to the Corinthians*, Grand Rapids: William B. Eerdmans Publishing Co., 1987.

*The Great Ideas: A Syntopicon of Great Books of the Western World*, Chicago: William Benton, 1952.

Gregory, Bishop of Nyssa, *On the Making of Man*, in *Nicene and Post-Nicene Fathers*, 2nd series, Peabody, MA: Hendrickson Publishers, 1995. [republished from 1892]

St. Gregory Nazinanzen, "On the Holy Spirit" as *The Fifth Theological Oration*, in *Nicene and Post-Nicene Fathers*, 2nd series, Peabody, MA: Hendrickson Publishers, 1995. [republished from 1892]

Gregory of Nyssa, *On the Making of Man*, sec. V, in *Nicene and Post-Nicene Fathers*, 2nd series, Peabody, MA: Hendrickson Publishers, 1995. [republished from 1892]

Gregory of Nyssa, *On the Soul and the Resurrection*.

*A Greek-English Lexicon*, 8th ed., comp. by Henry G. Liddell and Robert Scott, New York: American Book Co., 1897.

http://www.ntgreek.org/learn_nt_greek/verbs.htm.

http://www.foundalis.com/lan/grkverbs.htm.

*Harper's Bible Dictionary*, San Francisco: Harper & Row, 1985.

Harvey, William, *Animal Generation*, Chicago: William Benton, 1952. [republished translation by Robert Willis in 1847]

Hastings, James, *Dictionary of the Bible*, New York: Charles Scribner's Sons, 1937.

Hegel, Georg Wilhelm Friedrick, "The German World," *Philosophy of History*, The Reformation," "The Modern Time," Chicago:

William Benton, 1952. [republished translation of 1858 by J. Sibree, rev. 1899]

*The Interpreter's Bible*, New York: Abingdon-Cokesbury Press, 1952.

*The Interpreter's Dictionary of the Bible*, Nashville: Abingdon Press, 1962.

Jacobus, Melancthon W., *et al.*, *A Standard Bible Dictionary*, New York: Funk & Wagnalls Co., 1909.

James, William *Principles of Psychology*, Chicago: William Benton, 1952.

Jamieson, Robert, A.R. Fausset, and David Brown, *A Commentary, Critical and Explanatory, on the Old and New Testaments*, I, Hartford: S.S. Scranton, 1872.

St. Jerome, *Letter* LVIII, in *Nicene and Post-Nicene Fathers*, 2nd series, Peabody, MA: Hendrickson Publishers, 1995. [republished from 1892]

*Jewish Women Encyclopedia*: http://jwa.org/encyclopedia/article/rabbis-in-united-states.

John of Damascus, *Exposition of the Orthodox Faith*, in *Nicene and Post-Nicene Fathers*, 2nd series, Peabody, MA: Hendrickson Publishers, 1995. [republished from 1892]

Johnson, Allan G., *The Gender Knot: Unraveling Our Patriarchal Legacy*, rev. and updated ed., Philadelphia: Temple University Press, 2005.

Johnson Luke Timothy, *The Apostle Paul*, a course guidebook, Chantilly, Virginia: The Teaching Company, 2001.

King, Karen L., *The Gospel of Mary of Magadala: Jesus and the First Woman Apostle*, Santa Rosa: Polebridge Press, 2003.

Locke, John, *Concerning Human Understanding*, Chicago: William Benton, 1952. [republished from the sixteen hundreds]

Lowes, John Livingston, *The Road to Xanadu: A Study in the Ways of the Imagination*, Sentry ed., Boston: Houghton Mifflin, 1964.

MacDonald, Margaret Y., *Early Christian Women and Pagan Opinion*, Cambridge, England: Cambridge University Press, 1996.

Melville, Herman, *Moby Dick; or, The Whale*, Chicago: William Benton, 1952. [republished from 1851]

Mollenkott, Virginia Ramey, *The Divine Feminine: The Biblical Imagery of God as Female*, New York: Crossroad, 1983. (See this theology professor's book also for other feminine references to God that I have not covered.)

National Council of the Churches of Christ, *An Inclusive Language Lectionary: Readings of Year A*, Philadelphia: The Westminster Press, 1983.

*The New Testament and Psalms: An Inclusive Version*, New York, New York: Oxford University Press, 1995.

Newton, Isaac, *Mathematical Principles*, Chicago: William Benton, 1952. [republished translation by André Motte in 1729, revised by Florian Cajori (1859-1930), and copyrighted by The Regents of The University of California in 1934, renewed in 1962]

Noble, David F., *A World Without Women*, New York: Alfred A. Knopf, 1992.

Osiek, Carolyn, Margaret Y. MacDonald, and Janet H. Tulloch, *A Woman's Place: House Churches in Earliest Christianity*, Minneapolis: Fortress Press, 2006.

*The Oxford English Dictionary, The Compact Edition*, vol. II, New York: Oxford University Press, 1971.

Patai, Raphael, *The Hebrew Goddess*, 3rd enlarged ed., Detroit: Wayne State University Press, 1978.

PBS's *NOVA* DVD, *The Bible's Buried Secrets: Beyond Fact or Fiction*, 2009.

PBS DVD "Three Faiths, One God: Judaism, Christianity, Islam, Part I," 2002.

PBS's DVD *When Worlds Collide: The Untold Story of the Americas after Columbus*, 2010.

Plato's *Republic*, trans. by Francis Cornford, London: Oxford University Press, 1941.

Plotinus, *Third Ennead*, Chicago: William Benton, 1952. [republished translation (originally 1917-1930) by Stephen MacKenna and B. S. Page]

Rohm, Robert A., *Positive Personality Profiles*, Atlanta: Personality Insights, 1994.

Santmire, H. Paul, "Retranslating 'Our Father': the Urgency and the Possibility," *Dialog*, 1977.

Scofield, C. I., *The Scofield Reference Bible*, new and improved ed., New York: Oxford University Press, 1917.

Scofield, C. I., *The Scofield Reference Bible*, New York: Oxford University Press, 1945.

Shakespeare, William, *Macbeth*.

Smith, William, *A Dictionary of the Bible*, Hartford: S.S. Scranton, 1868.

Stone, Merlin, *When God Was a Woman*, New York: Barnes & Noble, 1993.

Strauss, Mark L., *Distorting Scripture? The Challenge of Bible Translation & Gender Accuracy*, Downers Grove, IL: InterVarsity Press, 1998.

Tan, Paul Lee, *The Interpretation of Prophecy*, Winona Lake, IN: BMH Books, 1974.

Tolstoy, Leo, *War and Peace*, Chicago: William Benton, 1952. [republished translation by Louise Maude (1855-1939) and Aylmer Maude (1858-1938)]

Torjesen, Karen Jo, *When Women Were Priests: Women's Leadership in the Early Church & the Scandal of Their Subordination in the Rise of Christianity*, New York: HarperOne, 1993.

Trench, Richard, *The Parables of Our Lord*, London: Macmillan, 1882.

Wilder, Thornton, *Three Plays: Thornton Wilder*, New York: Bantam Books, 1957.

Wills, Garry, *Papal Sin: Structures of Deceit*, New York: Doubleday, 2000.

Printed in the United States
by Baker & Taylor Publisher Services